Living in the Comfort Zone

The Gift of Boundaries in Relationships

ROKELLE LERNER

Health Communications, Inc.
Deerfield Beach, Florida

Library of Congress Cataloging-in-Publication Data

Lerner, Rokelle.
    Living in the comfort zone : the gift of boundaries in rela-
tionships / by Rokelle Lerner.
        p. cm.
    Includes bibliographical references.
    ISBN 1-55874-370-7
    1. Personal space—Psychological aspects. 2. Boundaries—
Psychological aspects. 3. Self. 4. Identity (Psychology) 5.
Interpersonal relations. 6. Interpersonal relations—Religious
aspects. I. Title.
BF697.L396 1995
158'.2—dc20   95-42236
                                                          CIP

©1995 Rokelle Lerner
ISBN 1-55874-370-7

Publisher: Health Communications, Inc.
               3201 S.W. 15th Street
               Deerfield Beach, Florida 33442-8190

Cover design by Andrea Perrine Brower

To my beloved teachers,
who opened my heart and allowed
me to learn about boundaries
most profoundly.

A *healthy well-established boundary*
is an internalized limit, physical, emotional,
intellectual, spiritual, that enhances a
sense of identity by implanting more deeply
the precious knowledge that one is
a separate human being.

CONTENTS

Foreword.. xi

Acknowledgments xiii

Introduction xv

A Parable xxiii

1. Life in the Comfort Zone 1

2. Creating a Safe Container: Developing Boundaries.... 11

3. The Plan for Growth 27

4. The Dance of Attachment and Kathy's Story 39

5. Boundary Violations and John's Story.......................... 57

6. All or Nothing at All: The Dynamics of
   Intrusion and Distancing... 83

7. Rules, Regulations and Consciousness:
   Creating a Sacred Reality... 95

8. The Decision to Heal 109

9. Boundaries for All Occasions: Creativity in Action...119

10. Mending Body and Soul 129

11. Hold That Feeling and I'll Express It for You:
     Projective Identification and Bonding Patterns..........145

12. Relationships: The Most Rigorous Spiritual Path.......159

13. Heart and Soul: Love's True Journey...........................175

Appendix...187

Bibliography 189

FOREWORD

As Rokelle Lerner so beautifully illustrates in *Living in the Comfort Zone*, the world exists by virtue of its boundaries. It used to be that these boundaries were very clear. Day was day, night was night, good was good and bad was bad. Today the world suffers from a loss of boundaries.

When we have no boundaries, the way we conduct our lives depends on how we feel at the time. That's not sanity; that's insecurity. A person isn't secure because he thinks well of himself; a person is secure because he knows what he needs to be doing.

In this book, Ms. Lerner carefully identifies the most important boundary, that framework that makes us who we are, that gives to us a sense of separateness and a sense of stability: *morality*.

If we know what we may do and what we may not, that's our boundary. But more than that, Ms. Lerner emphasizes, morality is what gives us a *sense of self*.

Living in the Comfort Zone reminds us that selfhood is created not by our opinions of ourselves but by seeking a clarity of private versus public, appropriate versus inappropriate, allowed versus not allowed, and especially, right versus wrong. Rokelle Lerner has given us meaningful insights, both practical and spiritually healing, into the timeless code by which the world endures.

—Rabbi Manis Friedman

Rabbi Friedman is the author of Doesn't Anyone Blush Anymore? Reclaiming Intimacy, Modesty, and Sexuality, *the host of a nationally syndicated television series,* Organic Conversation with Manis Friedman, *and founder and dean of Bais Chana Institute in St. Paul. He is known throughout the world as a philosopher, lecturer, and family counselor.*

ACKNOWLEDGMENTS

During the last six years many friends and professional colleagues have helped me turn concepts into the reality of a finished book.

- To Roy Carlisle of Mills House, my editorial consultant, who provided his talent and continual encouragement. I knew that we had a book that was worth waiting for!
- To John Archer I give a special note of appreciation for his wealth of information.
- To Audrey DeLaMartre, my wonderful editor, whose enthusiasm was contagious!
- To Dr. Goldie Antelman and Dr. Glenna Schroeder, whose brilliance I acknowledge and who I thank for their willingness to explore this subject with me in depth.
- To Dr. Angeles Arrien whose inspirational work helped me to form the conceptual basis for the healing work on boundaries.

- To Lori Dwinell, my thanks for her wisdom and expertise.
- To Mary Stangler and Carol Magee who helped me organize my thoughts in patient and wonderful ways.
- To Lois Weisberg who added clarity to this book through her command of language.
- To Lori Banker whose assistance was far beyond valuable.
- To my daughters, Meredith and Sasha Lerner, who got to hear about this book *ad nauseum* for lo these many years.
- To the men and women who allowed me to tell their stories. It is because of their generosity that others may take hope for their own healing journeys.

INTRODUCTION

Wouldn't it be wonderful to live in a world where people related with respect and even reverence for all living things? This would inspire us to honor others with a personal sacred space of respect beyond which we would not intrude by word or deed. Without that safety, we will be unable to bring the sacred and the spiritual into our relationships.

The term *comfort zone* describes that internal place of sanctuary that we create by developing and maintaining our boundaries. It is that internal sacred space that provides us with protection and solace, and enables us to find a sense of well-being that we can carry with us everywhere.

It's very hard to establish an inner sanctuary if the self is unknown. So in some ways this book is a challenge to explore the unknown depths of soul and claim the totality of who we are. Only then can we experience a state of consciousness that allows us to soothe ourselves with the precious knowledge that we are separate, and yet infinitely connected.

Through our conscious creation of boundaries we will develop the ability to establish a sacred container from which to contemplate our oneness. Without this knowledge we will turn desperately to anything that can medicate our dis-ease.

Boundaries allow us to feel safe in our world filled with personalities, demands and pressures. A *comfort zone* is the internal experience of peace and boundless connection that cannot easily be realized without boundaries. Meditation, yoga, prayer and other spiritual practices are useful in creating this place of comfort. But for some of us, these become only techniques and temporary solutions, particularly if we are victims or perpetrators.

Of course, there are those extraordinary people who have been able to create an inner sanctuary even while tolerating hideous violation. From prisoners of war to holocaust survivors, history is filled with incredible stories that testify to the mind's ability to go to any length to keep us from our pain. Others may dissociate—become psychologically not-present—and escape from their present experiences.

However, we need to be present in body, mind and spirit to create healthy relationships. We need to develop the capacity to be fully present, *and* still have the ability to access our internal sacred space where we can experience rejuvenation, calm, objectivity and the knowing of who we are. For that reason this book addresses both the practical issues of maintaining our separateness and the sacred domain of connection. This is not a duality, but a continuum of the whole. We must learn to bring the sacred in our everyday interactions and walk a spiritual path with practical feet.

Relationships are learning labs for the development of boundaries. It is through relationships that we are inspired and literally propelled to move out of our narrow definitions of self and meet those disowned parts that can contaminate all of our relationships. With the light of love we can illumine those dark places of fear, anger and abandonment. When we know how these feelings are triggered, then we can have choices about how we contain, react or respond to others. Until we open the doors to those unknown places of our souls, we will continue to do violence to others and to our planet. We will collectively and unknowingly project our rage and our fear in ways that collectively will destroy our civilization as we know it.

Without developing healthy boundaries we all have the potential to destroy as well as create. Without a comfort zone we are too busy defending ourselves to understand the presence of the sacred in all things. This has never been more evident than today. All we need to do is walk out our doors at night or turn on the television to witness the absence of the sacred in our interactions with others. We have become so conditioned to the illusion that the ability to violate exists outside of us, that we have abdicated responsibility for our actions. Fundamentalists would say that the devil is always lurking in our world, ready to influence us at every turn. While certainly we could blame the world's travails on the devil, I find more realistic what Mohandas Ghandi said: "The only devils running rampant are the devils within our own hearts." If humanity is to survive, it's imperative that we recognize how each of us contributes to the violence in the world and learn how to change our responses. It's time for *all* of us to manifest discipline and intentionality in *all* our interactions.

Several years ago, Soviet politician Mikhail Gorbachev said to then President Reagan something that was overlooked by most people. He said that the USSR was going to do something devastating to the United States: that Russia was "going to take the enemy away." It's tragic to realize that for communities to thrive, enemies have been just as important as friends. When we can project our disowned rage and terror on an enemy outside of us, it brings out the qualities of self-sacrifice and group cohesion. Without boundaries to contain our rage, without a comfort zone in which to experience the sacred, we may all be doomed to experience the violence that pervades our culture. As cartoon character Pogo said, "We have met the enemy, and they is us!"

When first I heard of the concept of physical, emotional and intellectual boundaries, I thought that it was a theory created by bored graduate students, who sat around between Pavlovian seminars discussing what was new with the rats. As time went on, I noticed that boundaries was a word used often in recovery vernacular. People used this term to explain a host of situations from painful relationships to problems at work. I have a funny habit of questioning the value of a term that describes everything from indigestion to menopause. What started as casual curiosity to investigate the etiology of this term turned out to be a psychological and spiritual journey that led to the development of this book.

As it turned out, boundary problems do indeed impact personal and professional relationships of every kind. This word encompasses dynamics of interaction from the family dinner table to the Israeli-Palestinian negotiating table. The unavailability of emotional, physical and intellectual boundaries helps to explain the violence that pervades our culture, as well as our inability to form relationships that are life-enhancing rather than life-draining.

Nothing is more important in our lives than our connections with other humans. Yet, for all our advancement in science and technology, we still don't know how to get along with one another. Everywhere we turn there seems to be a glut of books and seminars on healing relationships. We are finally catching on that a dynamic part of healing Mother Earth is attending to what is happening between people. Truly, all the recycling efforts won't save this planet unless we pay attention to the ecology of relationships. *The worldwide violence and destruction is a macrocosm of individual relationships.* For that reason it's crucial to heal our boundaries and create our own inner sanctuaries. It is no longer a luxury, it's a *necessity.* The most profound way to do this is to develop our own comfort zones with the intention of learning how to feel at home with ourselves and experience safety with others emotionally, physically and eventually spiritually. We need to examine all our relationships, including our relationship to Mother Earth. Only then can we discover how to maintain deep connections with others that are whole, healthy and life-giving. Only then can we restore our planet to health.

In this book I address two primary questions that allow loving connections to thrive. First, how can I maintain my sense of self and still be in relationship with another person? Then as we long to go deeper into the spirituality of relating, the second question becomes, how do I bring forward respect and the intrinsic sacred in my relationships when the conflict and stress of everyday life occurs?

It seems a paradox to join autonomy with intimacy. It's even more paradoxical to think of holding in mind the idea of our partner's fundamental sacredness when we're so angry that we could induce a meltdown! While we don't have to sacrifice one state of mind to embrace the other, some of us have done just that.

We haven't been given healthy models that have shown us how to stay in a relationship with mutuality and personal integrity when the initial romance wears thin. Others can't discern when it's time to leave a relationship and tolerate hideous abuse because their boundaries are practically nonexistent. The only examples we have for relationships come usually from our parents. For many, this is not exactly the ideal, loving relationship to inspire us.

In our society we tend to view relationships as a fix for loneliness and quickly become disenchanted when opportunities arise for us to really learn about our boundaries in a most profound way. For this reason it's crucial that we broaden our view of relationships to reach far beyond the initial romantic phase. We need a new vision of sustained relating that brings us into the quality of healing that only the power of love can manifest.

Most of us hold childlike images of relationships that we learned from myth and fairy tales. Although these stories are rich in metaphor, it's helpful to remember that most heroines had questionable boundaries. Snow White, for example, is about a young woman who was kicked out of her home by an abusive, narcissistic (alcoholic? we will never know) stepmother who daily talked to her mirror. Meanwhile in an attempt to escape, Snow White focuses her attention on a group of seven asexual little men, each with a major personality flaw. She takes good care of them, but eventually waits for some necrophile in the woods, in this case, a man who will kiss a dead woman in the forest. Some story! Certainly not one that teaches healthy boundaries or relationships. Are you sure you want to read such a bedtime story to your children?

In an age where the various media influence our judgment, it's easy to be confused about the two very different experiences of falling in love and of sustaining a long-term relationship. Often we're shown the lovely, romantic phase of a relationship, but never get to see what happens if the couple makes a decision to turn romance into a conscious growth-fostering relationship. There is no doubt why so many couples who experience the normal ebb of romance want to throw in the towel and call it quits. Far too often, if the couple gets beyond the romance stage, the story becomes one of violence in some form. Some get right to work on the day to day business of earning a living or sharing housework and never create an inspiring shared vision. Falling in love is the wonderful fire that invites us into the real soul work of relationships. Whether we accept the invitation is up to us.

Many readers are psychologically sophisticated already, but understanding concepts is only a small part of the challenge. Putting them into action takes far more. That's why sometimes it takes a blasting wake-up call to get us to focus our attention and move into understanding our boundaries deeply, body, mind and spirit. Sometimes our awakening is delivered in a form that is so wounding that it forces us to change how we exist in the world. Often it takes deep love and loss that cracks open our hearts so profoundly that integrity, identity and spirituality finally emerge. Through this kind of awakening many of us give birth to what Native Americans would call our sacred hoop, a comfort zone that previously we could only intellectualize but never quite experience.

For all of us, the healing and reclaiming of our boundaries enriches our lives with a greater measure of safety and serenity. Like anything else in life that is worthwhile, this work takes practice, persistence, commitment and courage. I wish for you the strength to sustain your work, even when the going gets tough. I invite you to borrow hopefulness from others who have walked through that darkness of despair and confusion, and out the other side. The many gifts that will manifest through your efforts will be beyond your wildest imagination!

A PARABLE

---

*The more carefully we listen to the
voice inside of us, the more clearly we will
hear what is sounding outside.*

Dag Hammarskjöld

Many years ago, in old Hungary, there was a monastery
whose numbers had greatly diminished, until only three
brothers remained. They had lost respect for themselves and
the monastery and people no longer came to worship. The
grounds of the monastery that once were beautiful were run-
down. The brothers looked slovenly and unhappy. They
seemed like strangers living together and the mood of the
monastery was one of isolation and cool indifference. Yet,

they were all worried about the future of the abbey, so they prayed and meditated each day.

It came to pass that an old wise woman was passing through the village, looking for a place to meditate and be in silence. This village looked so quiet that she decided to settle in a hut near the woods for her meditation retreat. One day the monks encouraged the abbot to visit the wise woman and ask her advice about what they might do to save their community. They were all getting older and soon there would be no one left.

The wise woman greeted the abbot and fixed a pot for them. All day they talked about life and God. Toward evening, as he was leaving, the abbot remembered the reason for his visit, that he was to ask the wise woman how they might save their little community. The old crone said that she didn't know, but she could tell him this, *one* of them was the Messiah.

Excited, the abbot returned to his community to tell his fellow monks the incredible news. They discussed the amazing news in great excitement, and found that not one of them could quite bring himself to believe that one of them might actually be the Messiah.

Possibly, they thought, the Messiah might be brother Joseph, as he was the most pious of them all. He was the choir master and had a beautiful voice. But he was quite timid, spent most of his time at prayer and spoke rarely. He avoided visitors and disliked interruptions to his daily routine. How could such a shy, retiring person possibly be the Messiah?

And how could it possibly be brother Andrew, the cook for the monastery? He was very overweight and always complained that not enough work was getting done. He laid heavy burdens and demands on the other brothers while he was lazy about his own chores. Surely it was not demanding Andrew.

But neither could it be brother Philip. He was the gardener and something of a mister fix-it, but he was also given to temper tantrums. They could always depend on Philip to be there in times of trouble, but sometimes he lost his temper and used profanities. Surely the Messiah wouldn't be someone who threw temper tantrums!

They could not figure out who the Messiah might be. Nevertheless, on the *chance* that one of them might be the Messiah, they started treating each other with respect.

Each man wondered to himself if it were possible that, in some miraculous way, he might indeed by the Messiah. So it happened that each man also began to treat *himself* more respectfully. Joseph became more outgoing and willing to speak to others. Andrew eased up on complaining and began to take more responsibility. Philip gained noticeable control over his temper.

There definitely was a positive feeling about the whole community. The brothers were kinder and more respectful to each other and they all worked harder than ever to make improvements in the buildings and gardens of the monastery. Passersby remarked that their chants had become more melodic and even their prayers were more devout.

Before long the people from the village heard about the improvements in the monastery and came to see what was going on. Soon their reputation for piety and kindness, the sweetness of their chants and the increasing beauty of their gardens began to spread. More and more visitors came. In the evening people came just to walk through the garden and sit in the chapel to listen to the monks chant vespers.

Then one day it happened that one of the young men who was visiting asked if he might become a novice. News of the miracles at the monastery spread to other towns and villages and people from all over the country began to make pilgrimages to the monastery. Every now and then another young man joined the community and slowly the monastery grew.

After several years had passed, the brothers, who had grown in wisdom, announced to the community that the Messiah was one of them. With that news the younger brothers began to treat each other with more respect and reverence. And to this very day there continues to exist a thriving monastic community in that village in old Hungary.[1]

---

1. This lovely little piece, given to me by a friend, was published anonymously and entitled "The Rabbi."

CHAPTER

1

Life in the Comfort Zone

---

*"What lies before us and what lies
behind us, are but small matter compared to
what lies within us. And when we bring
what is within out into the world,
miracles happen."*

Henry David Thoreau

Few of us in our western culture know where our comfort zone is. Indeed, *what* it is probably provokes some confusion. We are raised to live the American Way, the way of the warrior, the pioneer, the manifest entrepreneur. This has served us well for centuries! To go where no one has gone before, to paraphrase *Star Trek*, helped our foreparents to stretch beyond their limits, to find new territory, new ways of solving old problems and conquering new ones. Now it seems that what we haven't learned is how to be inside our bodies. How ironic that in this advanced society we've created we don't know how to live with ourselves and each other. This phenomenon creates a tragic disparity as we continue stretching outward, conquering and creating. The disparity that exists is the incredible potential that we have created by our progress, and our inability to participate in that potential.

3

With all our technology, where do we find a sense of ease? Is it in our homes? Most people say no. Is it at work, with friends, with our family, lovers or in nature? Most of us truly don't have a place that provides us with a sense of sanctuary. We feel we must always be vigilant. In fact, this predicament was foretold by authors of Utopian literature. For example, in his book *1984* George Orwell suggests that there would be no place of refuge because "Big Brother" was everywhere watching, lurking, waiting.[1] And what was the solution suggested for the populace in Huxley's *Brave New World?*[2] They could find comfort in "soma," a drug dispensed to the entire population that took all the edges off emotions, let them forget problems and provided a comforting sense of well-being. Sound familiar? Today few of us know at least one person who is *not* on Prozac or some other psychotropic.

It would be irresponsible to omit that many people have literally been saved by these kinds of anti-depressants. However, I propose that many folks have been prescribed this drug to quell an ongoing anxiety that reveals an unwillingness to be in one's skin, a fear of a world that is filled with abuse, violence and sexually transmitted diseases, an easier cure for a malady that affects the whole of society. After all, it's much easier to take a pill than to go through the labor of trusting our senses and making decisions based on our integrity. If pills or machines could fix our intimate relationships or make us better parents, most of us would be lined up at the drug counters.

The problem is that in those quiet moments, in those times when we can't sleep, we still feel the emptiness, the aloneness, the void and sometimes the terror. For in the last

1. George Orwell, *1984* (New York: Knopf, 1992).
2. Aldus Huxley, *Brave New World* (New York: Harper Collins, 1932).

analysis, we all must go through the effort of finding ourselves and waking our senses if we are to have any sense of security and feel at home with Mother Earth. There aren't enough weapons, burglar alarms, mace cans or technological ingenuity that can do it for us. That's why there's a renewed interest in the spirituality of indigenous cultures. These less technological people felt at home where they were, they lived with the rhythm of Earth's seasons, they knew and depended on their bodies, and they felt the presence of the sacred in all life forms. With the growth of our technology we lost that connection to the sacred. Now we wonder what happened to us.

Many cultures have rituals for children entering adulthood, moving from a separate entity into a responsible member of the community. Children in many cultures—for example, Native American, Maoris, Basque and so on— were exposed to rigorous study of the self and the culture through vision quests, shamanic journeys and intensive study. Children were allowed and virtually pushed to find a sense of themselves and their purpose, before joining the collective community. In our society we are rarely, if ever, given the opportunity of such ritual. Today, the rites of passage from adolescence to adulthood are getting a driver's license, getting drunk or getting pregnant. How do we teach adolescents to find their comfort zone when we are so confused about our own?

As we move into this twenty-first century, the challenge we face is to achieve a balance between technology and our need to return to a sense of comfort. Not the kind of comfort that money buys or pharmaceuticals create, but the kind of ease and comfort we feel when we're attuned to our thoughts, our feelings and our bodily responses. The kind of security and well-being we experience when we learn to heed the signals we get from our bodies and our environment. Only then can we exist on this planet with understanding, wisdom and discernment. If this were the case now, we wouldn't have to teach children to "just say no," or to teach women that they don't have to tolerate violence in their relationships. We are being called on to move from reaction to creation. As anthropologist Angeles Arrien says, "It is easy to discuss what the problem is and complain, it is much more difficult to use our internal wisdom to create solutions."[3] This is partially why those in the recovery movement are becoming less interested in describing the problems of their dysfunctional families, and are instead searching for solutions that can bring forward their spirituality, wisdom, safety and ongoing sense of comfort on this planet.

When is the last time you felt a sense of well-being and ease? Many of us look back to some childhood memory when we were free from responsibility, when we could run or jump or skip and let the wind blow through our hair. Some of us remember being held or touched or tucked into bed by loving adults who assured us that the world would still be there in the morning. Some of us never achieved this kind of comfort until adulthood, if ever! If you can remember a time when you felt a sense of comfort, write it down and try to recall what the circumstances were. What was the lighting, the smell, the taste, the sound, the touch? How did your body feel? Where did you feel relaxation? These are the sensations within your comfort zone. It's a space that no one can take away from you and no one can enter unless you agree.

Now, think of a time when you walked right into hurt or danger. Did you have a sense that danger was approaching? Was there something inside of you that knew you shouldn't be walking down that street or starting that relationship or

3. Arrien, Angeles, "Human Resources: Doorways for Human Survival in the 21st Century." Presentation given at the Alternatives '94 conference.

taking that job or hanging around for the verbal abuse? As you recall this situation, remember how your body felt. Did you have a tight gut, were your palms sweaty, was your heart palpitating, was your mind racing or did you feel numb? These are all signals that you were about to violate your own boundaries and leave your comfort zone. If that's what you did, don't be too hard on yourself. Most of us were raised to ignore danger or violence, "damn the torpedoes, full speed ahead!" Especially women in our culture who are taught to please others, and men who are taught to ignore their pain. Daily we push ourselves beyond our limits, until we lose our way home. We overtax our endocrine system and then wonder why diseases of the immune system are rampant. Creating boundaries and a comfort zone that we know and can depend on isn't a trivial exercise, it's a matter of survival.

I suggest that we've moved our boundary lines so far away that they are almost irretrievable. Now we must go about the job of creating a sacred space for ourselves. That begins by realizing that we're separate from all other beings. Some who are spiritually sophisticated might balk and say, "That isn't true; we *are* all connected." I agree, but that protest misses an important step: we can't know connectedness with others without first knowing a sense of our own separateness. Any attempt at spiritualizing or intellectualizing this concept is folly without the important discovery of self. So many have tried to bypass this crucial step and have come to dire straits, from evangelists who are now imprisoned to New Age gurus who are now looking for methods to combat their depression.

Typically, when we feel there's something missing in our lives, what we're feeling is a spiritual deficiency, but we tend to search outside ourselves for ways to fill the aching void. Like orphans searching for homes, we chase frantically after anything that seems to offer a sense of security and peace. We lose our integrity, ignore our boundaries and become obsessed with shopping, eating, sex, exercise, drugs, new relationships and anything that looks appealing. Without an inner comfort zone, we seek solace anywhere. Ultimately, we learn the bitter lesson that these solutions are temporary at best, and eventually can lead to our demise. The irony is that when we slow down and develop a sense of inner comfort and well-being, we realize that what we were searching for outside was inside all along. Within each of us is the ability to cease the despair and create a true and enduring sanctuary. It is in the frantic desperation, the search for a quick fix that we lose ourselves.

A fable about a young pup and a very old dog conveys a lesson worth remembering. Every day the pup chased his tail frantically while the old dog watched with lazy amusement. The pup wanted the old dog to be his friend, but the wise old dog just told him to come back when he knew who he was and what he wanted. The pup continued to spend so much time and energy chasing his own tail that sometimes he would collapse in desperation. Sometimes he even lost his way home and feared he might spend the rest of his life chasing this thing that he wanted so much.

Several years later the weary dog turned to his older mentor for help. "I can't stand it anymore! Every time I think I finally have it, I lose it and have to run faster!" he complained.

The older dog smiled. "I have watched you run in circles for a long time. I knew that you were getting weaker and losing your spirit, but until you were ready to slow down and look at yourself, there was no use in saying anything!" Then he took his friend's small tail gently in his teeth and said, "Is this what you're looking for?"

The pup gasped. "How did you do that? It feels like it's mine!"

"It was yours all the time!" the older dog said. "But the more you chased after it, the more you got lost and tired and preoccupied. Go home now and rest. Tomorrow you will begin to know what is you and what isn't. Then we can be friends."

The time has come for each of us to move beyond our narrow or blurred definitions of self. It is time to move beyond lives filled with malaise, anxiety and discomfort. As the next millennium approaches, we must bring forward our commitment to exist within a *comfort zone*. It is time to create and heal our boundaries. Only then can we learn to co-exist with others in ways that won't drain us of vitality, integrity and dignity. Through this work we can know with profound certainty who we are and who we are not. Then we can know our soul, embrace our spirit, with enough self-knowledge that we can create relationships that will flourish.

CHAPTER

2

Creating a Safe Container: Developing Boundaries

Boundaries help to form that sacred container in which children can feel safe enough to discover themselves and the world. In order to have a sense of self-respect, ease and comfort wherever we go, it is imperative to know about our boundaries. Only by knowing and claiming our boundaries can we create a comfort zone, a sacred space in which we can do the soul work necessary to actualize our potential and still feel grounded in our identity.

All humans are born pre-programmed with the *ability* to develop and maintain their survival, personal protection and the continuation of their species. Whether we are speaking of Australian aborigines or Uptown Junior League women, each adult on every continent is morally charged with the responsibility for teaching children what they must or must not do to find comfort, safety and eventually a sense of themselves.

Although this comparison may be drastic, the survival of most cultures depends on individuals who claim their identity and become the culture-bearers of their society.

Ironically, only through understanding or awareness of self can we seriously pursue the meaning of our lives and the ways our spirit can seek oneness with the greater Source. It is virtually impossible to claim our boundaries and establish our identity when there is no protection or safety to do so. For this reason it has become increasingly clear to theologians, psychologists and anthropologists that establishing safety, identity and spirituality demands some knowledge of internal and external boundaries. We can't skip over, intellectualize or spiritualize this issue. We cannot borrow someone else's boundaries, identity or spirituality. So, the good news is that we *get to* do this ourselves, in our own way and in our own time. The challenge is that we *must* do this ourselves, and unfortunately cannot hire a helping professional or spiritual teacher to do it for us. Years of psychoanalysis or religious training may help us to understand boundaries, but as history demonstrates understanding isn't enough. Some of the most hideous violations have been committed in the name of God or in the name of counter transference. The news is filled with abuse violations committed by professionals who may understand the concepts around boundaries, but who continue to violate those they serve.[1]

Unfortunately, a person without boundaries is like a country without laws. Without boundaries, we can be robbed, violated, seduced or ignored without ever knowing why. Boundaries help to form the safe container in which our identity develops. Our likes and dislikes, the intensity of emotion we can bear, the clarity of our ideas, all depend upon

---

1. Marilyn Peterson, *At Personal Risk* (New York: Norton, 1992).

the kinds of boundaries we create, or are created for us. Whether the formation process is healthy or seriously impaired, we are the final expert on our boundaries. The most important ground rule for those who are beginning this journey of healing is to create a margin of safety. For example, if someone tries to dictate where our limits are by touching or speaking inappropriately, or being more aggressive, it is time to exit quickly. If we don't, we're implying that it's acceptable to invade our boundaries. When we surrender our knowledge of self to another, however limited our knowledge may be, we are vulnerable to those who would violate our bodies, our psyches and literally rob our souls. No one, *no one* knows what boundaries or healing schedule are appropriate for another. That decision to heal is strictly personal and comes from within. We may need coaching and support from those around us, but the decision to heal is individual and often is inspired by a painful revelation showing that we must change our manner of presence in the world.

Carl Jung says that "you can't individuate on Mt. Everest!" The experience of transformation is a personal experience, but healing boundaries is a relational experience. Boundaries are formed in relationship and healed in relationship, so we can't lock ourselves in a closet and repair our boundaries. We need other people in order to develop a sense of ourselves. Solitude, reflection and contemplation are valuable, but we can't meditate our way to an earthly identity.

Since boundaries describe the totality of our identity, they can be physical, emotional, intellectual and even spiritual. The word boundary may bring to mind a physical limit, the edge of a lot, the border of a country, a written statute of limitations. External boundaries are sometimes as clear as a drawn line, but internal boundaries of self are neither visible nor touchable. Sue Evans envisions internal boundaries, describing a psychic bubble that helps separate us from each other.[2] In their insightful book *Facing Shame*, Merle Fossam and Marilyn Mason define an internal boundary as an "ego barrier that guards an individual's inner space."[3] My working definition is:

A healthy well-established boundary is an internalized limit, physical, emotional, intellectual, spiritual, that enhances a sense of identity by implanting more deeply the precious knowledge that one is a separate human being.

Physical boundaries define the margin of safety around our skin. They help to determine how close others may come to us, as well as how, when and where we want to be touched and by whom.

Emotional boundaries help us distinguish our own emotions from those of others, to recognize healthy expressions of our own feelings, and to take full responsibility for our behavior.

Intellectual boundaries allow us to process data from the outside world before it becomes part of our world view. Rather than waking every morning and letting the world happen to us, healthy intellectual boundaries make us proactive in relationship to our environment and help us to articulate our needs and desires.

Spiritual boundaries let us explore the possibilities of our existence: that in addition to our physical form, we are also spiritual beings, that we must walk a spiritual path with practical feet. Some say that we are acknowledging a Divine Consciousness from which all beings emanate. Others say that spiritual boundaries make us aware that we have the

---

2. Sue Evans, *Shame, Boundaries and Dissociation*, working paper.

3. Merle Fossom and Marilyn Mason, *Facing Shame: Families in Recovery* (New York: Norton, 1993), 63.

power to love and be loved. Whatever our preference, spiritual boundaries bridge an essential dimension of humanness connected to the ultimate source of love, however we might choose to define it.

To help prepare your mind and heart to receive what these pages offer, here is an affirmation that reflects the central theme of this book. Say each sentence to yourself slowly. Give yourself time to envision the truth each phrase contains, and savor how you feel as that truth takes root in you. As you let the words sink in no doubt you will have questions about their meaning. This book will help to answer some of those questions.

Given time and attention, your inner wisdom—that storehouse of truth that is profoundly accurate—will prevail. So find a quiet place, a still time, take a long, deep breath and begin by saying:

It is a loving thing to do to set my boundaries.
It is a loving thing to do to set my limits.
It is a statement about my dignity.
And the dignity I have for other people.

In order to discover the factors necessary to create a "safe container," it is imperative to look at the manner in which humans develop. I'm aware that the phrase *human development* has been known to trigger deep relaxation or even sleep, and I know that human development experts Piaget and Erikson aren't a fun nights reading! However, let's consider what it means when someone suggests that we *act our age*.

Child and adult developmental stages are established by a miraculous internal time clock in every human of every culture that sounds its alarm at distinct, preset stages. At two we say *no* and at three we ask *why*. At six we start questioning the rules and hassling our parents. Research has shown that this time clock must be respected and honored to allow individuals to flourish. Our primary caregivers are most critical for stimulating us to grow into and through our different stages of personality and functioning in human interaction.

The first job of a parent that most profoundly affects the development of healthy boundaries is *mirroring*. Our sense of who we are is shaped by this important process. Infants need parents who are clear mirrors that reflect back to them their physical and emotional essence. "Hello blue eyes!" or "I can see how you love to eat," or even mirroring infants' facial expressions and gazing into their eyes gives them a secure sense that they are known and loved. Those of us who were raised with parents who were withdrawn, depressed, disconnected or preoccupied with their own pain, received minimal feedback and distorted mirroring. Having parents with cloudy or distorted mirrors leads to blurred boundaries and narcissistic wounds later in life. These are adults who find and fuse with a partner in their desperate longing to know who they are. Some adults need that mirroring so much that they demand attention or admiration even if it means violating their own boundaries to get it.

Susan is a woman who suffers the effects of non-mirroring parents. She was raised by a chronically depressed mother and a father who was preoccupied with his wife's depression. Because Susan didn't receive adequate mirroring in childhood, as an adult she tends to seek attention and admiration from all her relationships. The people closest to her tire quickly of her constant attempts to solicit comments about her hair, her clothes, how she speaks, even how she drives a car. Intimate relationships cause her insurmountable pain because of her constant need for approval.

Susan feels good when her partner is pleased, and she feels bad when her partner is not pleased. When her partner is responsive Susan feels attractive, when her partner is not responsive she feels ugly. If her partner had a lousy day, Susan takes his mood as a reflection of herself and gets anxious. Her identity depends on how she is mirrored. Usually she gets involved with men who have complementary wounds and they both become hostile and dependent. Since their core needs are the same, neither one of them can ever be satisfied.

Parents and caregivers are essential also for boundary development. Infants aren't born with boundaries, but they are born with the mental equipment to develop boundaries. The relationship between parent and child allows or prohibits children from forming those essential edges. The parent-child relationship is that magical dance of development that pivots delicately around the balance between attachment and separation. In healthy families, parents learn to pick up cues that their children need to be held, touched, soothed, fed or even left alone. When parents respect and honor these signals, children learn to honor what their bodies are telling them and are able to set limits based on their physical and emotional integrity.

However, when children's signals are ignored, rejected or shamed, the result is a dissociative numbness that doesn't diminish with time or maturity. How many times can a child be cuddled and hugged against her will before she goes numb and submits? If Jimmy's hunger cries are ignored, or if his caregivers yell or terrorize him when he wants to eat, he may learn to ignore his body's hunger signals, distorting for a lifetime his relationship with food. I have worked with women and men who literally don't know that they are hungry until their blood sugar gets so low that it's painful. We must be embodied, in our bodies, to know our limits.

When we learn to ignore our body cues, we can't possibly get our needs met in ways that preserve our integrity. This applies particularly to the painful ways we undermine ourselves in relationships. Like a person who ignores sensations in her hand and continues to touch a hot stove, we put our-selves in danger when we learn to deny our physical signals. For example, Anna's mother was ill with a chronic condition that required her to medicate pain. As a child, Anna became vigilant about her mother's condition which was never fully explained to her. She learned that touch wasn't given based on her needs, but on her mother's energy level. The only time Anna had physical contact was when her mother unwittingly used Anna to comfort herself by holding Anna too close and too tightly.

Anna developed acute radar to recognize when her mother was available for closeness. She learned to ignore her own body cues and developed core beliefs about herself and the world that were based on her four-year-old assumptions. Anna grew up touch-starved, which was exacerbated by her belief that she could have closeness only when others wanted it. She believed that she had to accept touching in what ever manner it came to her. Her desperation and inability to read her own non-verbal cues led Anna to accept inappropriate and sometimes abusive physical contact by both men and women. Her childhood experience was truly the demise of Anna's physical boundaries.

Dr. Stanley Keleman describes Anna's painful dilemma:

> "Those of us who do not inhabit our flesh, who do not have the deep satisfaction that our bodies can give us, are always banging at the door of ourselves trying to get satisfaction. When we are afraid of our impulses, we lock ourselves in a world of ideas." [4]

I want to emphasize that Anna's mother was coping the only way she knew how and probably loved her daughter very

4. Stanley Keleman, *Your Body Speaks Its Mind* (Berkeley: Center Press, 1981), 31.

much. Ironically, boundaries are often destroyed in the name of love by parents who aren't aware of their own needs or their crucial role in their children's development. Boundaries first begin to form between three and six months, about the time when babies begin to realize that the arm carrying the spoon to feed them may not be their own! Before then, there is a natural blurring of boundaries between infants and parents, particularly mother. This symbiosis is beautiful to witness and characterizes a healthy relationship in the first few months of life. If you've ever watched a mother feed her baby, you've noticed that as the spoon filled with food approaches baby's mouth, mother's mouth opens too. However, if mother's mouth still opens and closes when her five-year-old eats a carrot, developmental sabotage is occurring! In other words, as children begin to individuate, parents must loosen the symbiotic tie too.

There are many studies describing what happens when infants aren't held and given adequate touch. Even though their basic needs are met, without that symbiotic bonding there's a high mortality rate and failure to thrive. Our very existence depends on this important attachment. It is the foundation of our being. Our developmental growth depends upon our ability to separate from our caregivers with a sense of security. How can we form boundaries and develop a sense of self if we have no parental object from which to separate? Conversely, how can we develop a separate identity from parents who never loosen that symbiotic tie? Many of us who didn't experience a healthy symbiotic tie, search the rest of our lives for the "good" mother or father who can fill the role for us. Sometimes, to the demise of our adult relationships. One of the biggest challenges of parenting is to be conscious of the delicate balance of attachment and separation throughout a child's life. Bigger still is developing that consciousness *before the child is born.*

At approximately 18 months, the lifelong dance of connection and disconnection is in full swing! As we grow into adulthood, the willingness to disconnect is an act of faith that is profoundly grounded or sabotaged at this crucial stage. This faith transcends all life's experiences and reassures us at a very deep level that we will wake again after sleep, that the person we love will return and that if we hold our breath, we will indeed breathe again.

At this stage, when children cuddle one minute and push away the next, parents can get bewildered. But this stage is crucial and children need parents who are consistent and loving. This is particularly challenging as kids experiment with their own power and anger. This often takes the form of *No! I won't! You can't make me!* In the Terrible Twos children must exercise their emotional and physical muscles that will be quite useful when they encounter peer pressure, experimentation with drugs or even violent acts or unwanted sex. To develop healthy boundaries we need to be able to display constructive anger, and in some homes, anger is a dangerous emotion to show. When children cannot assert themselves, they may develop damaging core beliefs that they carry throughout their lives:

To be angry is dangerous.
To be intruded upon is my duty.
To say no is disloyal.
If I separate, I'll lose love and affection.

I have found that those who don't have access to healthy displays of anger turn to whining instead, a sound that Mary Lee Zawadsky has described as "anger coming through a very small opening!"[5] If in adulthood we're still having whining

---

5. Mary Lee Zawadsky, *Experiential Approaches in Co-Dependency* (4th National Convention of Children of Alcoholics, 1988).

fits or tantrums, it's a sign that we still have two-year-old work to do. This work, whether done as a two-year-old or in adulthood, is the foundation of autonomy that determines our ability to say No! and is a powerful method of reclaiming boundaries. Psychologist Stanley Keleman writes eloquently about his fundamental statement:

"The ability to say no is the strongest expression of self-affirmation a child can make. If the assertion isn't respected, you get a 'no/body,' an amiable bowl of Jell-O who cannot accept the pleasure or pain that comes from risking, establishing distance from (parental) support."[6]

By the age of three, much of our primary boundary patterns are set. Yet parents need to honor a child's effort to separate or differentiate from them at every stage. That's how healthy families can help children act their age. There are no magic scissors to snip the steely ribbon of cultivated dependency at the age of 22. Nor are there dissolving agents that will melt those rigid walls that hold others away. If childrens' earliest efforts are not respected, they *never* become fully actualized adults. That is, they will never defy the gravitational pull of their families. It's as though an emotional umbilical cord ties them to their parents and chokes off their identity and stifles their spirit.

There's no doubt that what was created for us in child-hood, we live out in adulthood.[7] It's not hard to understand why some of us have problems creating a comfort zone that

---

6. Keleman, 33.

7. Pamela Levin, *Cycles of Power,* (Deerfield Beach, Florida: Health Communications, Inc., 1988).

provides us with the safety to know who we are and how we want to be treated. It's inevitable that issues and themes from childhood will return to us throughout our lives so that we can repair those mistaken assumptions and behaviors that have kept us rooted in misery. Instead of denying the fear and pain that these issues bring, we can learn to pay attention to our reactions and develop the important skill of discernment. Eventually we'll learn to know if we are reacting to our past or responding to the present. Childhood patterns can be released when we muster the courage and the willingness to change them. It's never too late to develop satisfying adult relationships that are based on our desire and integrity and not the unmet dependency needs of a small child.

As children, most of us had to surrender our timing to the adults around us. What we don't realize is what we had to do *internally* in order to carry out someone else's pattern of good behavior. It's probable that we had to contract our skeletal musculature, inhibit our peristaltic intestinal movement and even interfere with the rhythm of our heart and blood vessels! After learning such amazing control, these actions can actually prevent our ability now to reach out, run or even make noise.

That's why, to change childhood patterns, we must develop more than just an intellectual understanding of the problems. Our bodies are capable of re-learning if we become attuned to how we shape ourselves in relation to events and other people. When we can slow down and learn about our own rhythms, our own timing and our own laws, we can grasp finally the essence of real freedom. Developing our boundaries means that we can honor the natural ways we want to eat, breathe, walk down the street and even make love. We need to be conscious of how we adapt to other's timing by pulling in our shoulders, stiffening or squeezing our chest instead of asking someone to leave us alone.[8] The tasks of healing our boundaries are as complex as we are complex. Understanding the dynamics of boundary formation can help us to navigate the healing process. Keep in mind that success is a series of small changes and that the goal is obtainable. The work necessary to create a comfort zone sometimes is tedious, painful and even overwhelming. However, the results will strengthen our sense of self and enhance our ability to enter into loving, healthy relationships.

8. Stanley Keleman, *Somatic Reality*, (Berkeley: Center Press, 1979).

The Plan
for Growth

"Every seed must break its container,
otherwise there would
be no fruition."

Flora Maxwell

---

y life has been blessed with a close friend who is almost 70 years old. When we're together the age difference is insignificant. But occasionally, we become aware of the different eras of our birth. Ellie was born in 1925, the years of prohibition and speak-easies. Her mother and father, Scandinavian immigrants who were not affectionate with their children and kept their emotions to themselves, reacted to this era with a strict code of rules that naturally Ellie inherited. I was born in the 1948 post-war era, when families were enjoying freedom and prosperity after years of shortages, rationing and worrying about loved ones.

Ellie, a psychologist, lived with a woman for many years. Now she lives alone in a cabin she and her partner built in northern Minnesota. She is content with her life and I marvel at how the path she has chosen is so unlike her traditional

upbringing. Sometimes she describes her early years in high
school and college when she was living with the legacy of her
parents' view of the world. Her goal was to get a good education and marry a nice man who would take care of her. She
wasn't miserable about her fate. In fact, she assumed that this
is the way women were supposed to live, until her curiosity
allowed her to discover another whole world filled with color-
ful people who lived by their own rules. She made friends with
people from all walks of life and expanded her own world view.

Predictably, Ellie went through a rebellion where she cut
off her hair, quit school and experimented with alternative
lifestyles. She stepped out of her rigid physical and emotional
constraints and reveled in getting touch whenever she wanted
it. Her wake-up call came when she was in her late 20s
working at a mindless job and drinking herself into a stupor
each night. One morning she woke with such a hangover
that she couldn't get out of bed. She lay in her apartment for
two days feeling the emptiness that she could no longer medicate. It was clear that the choices she had made weren't
working for her. She started to remember her childhood
dream of creating a society where people could thrive. She
made a list of goals that she wanted and began to make a plan
to achieve those goals. Ellie sorted out what aspects of her life
she wanted to keep and what behaviors were not in her own
best interest.

She realized that she had been reacting to her parents'
strong value of education by dropping out of school, but actually she shared the value of education and returned to college
at age thirty. While she couldn't live with some of her family's
ideas about marriage, she knew that someday she wanted a
loving, committed relationship. She wasn't willing to go back
to the stoic physical boundaries of her childhood, but casual
sex and the intrusive touch from her friends, she realized, was
another reaction to her past, and not what she really wanted.

What she did in that room for those three days was to begin a conscious sorting process in which she kept the values, rules and boundaries that worked for her, and very intentionally discarded those that hurt, or didn't fit her.

Did she do it overnight? No. Was it an easy transition to make? It was the most challenging, difficult transition in her life. But what I notice now about Ellie is her sense of comfort and well-being that she carries wherever she goes. Living in her comfort zone, she has been able to give birth to her own spirituality that is rooted in her experience. Her life exemplifies the light at the end of the tunnel that is always attainable when we take responsibility for our lives and propel ourselves to action. Learning about her growth has been a marvelous catalyst for my own.

Clearly, there is a plan for growth in creating new boundaries. Becoming aware of this process can help those who are floundering in the sea of chaos known as transition. Our families transmit boundaries to us, and as we grow we react to these boundaries until we begin to internalize our own.

1. Transmitted Boundaries
These limits have an external form that may be a law, a moral principle, or an ethnic or family tradition. They are communicated intergenerationally through our families and institutions. Transmitted boundaries are also passed down culturally through song, myth and even fairy tales. No matter what the vehicle, transmitted boundaries coalesce in our unconscious and dictate how we are to be in the world physically and emotionally. These inherited limits are delivered to us at birth and come wrapped in rules or injunctions, expectations, unsaid innuendoes or gestures. Once internalized, they inform our conscience, and help to determine what we consider morally permissible.

Transmitted boundaries also form our attitudes about the

way things "ought to be." Some transmitted boundaries are virtually world-wide and can bridge centuries of human experience, such as the prohibition of willful murder. Others shift with time and circumstance, such as the expanded range of professional opportunity for American women and the resulting need to redefine our understanding of "women's work." Still others change through a deepening of consciousness or new understanding, like fresh legal interpretations about the crime of rape or heightened awareness of sexual harassment in the workplace. The power of these transmitted boundaries plays an integral role in our lives that often controls our future.

Religious and ethical doctrines are also a part of this group. They are handed down, often over centuries, through a variety of media—holy writings, solemn liturgies, hymns and prayers, community wisdom—and are generally administered by a caste of mediators set aside to be custodians of the sacred and dispensers of this wisdom.

Certain forms of transmitted or inherited boundaries are not productive and are stored in our unconscious while we unwittingly pass them down to our children. The no-talk rules in some families about sex or addiction, and the invisible loyalties that dictate our behavior in relationships are examples of transmitted boundaries.

An old story that illustrates our unquestioning acceptance of these inherited rules is about a young women who cut the ends off a ham whenever she baked it. When asked, she said she did it because her mother always did and so did her grandmother. One day she asked her grandmother why she cut the ends off her ham. "Because it's the only way I could fit it in the pot," grandmother replied.

2. Reactive Boundaries

Reactive boundaries grow out of internalized *responses* to transmitted boundaries. Our reaction to the boundaries we have inherited can provide us with the edge to achieve or the destiny to fail. For instance, a transmitted societal value dictates that "beautiful women get what they want." If this value also was communicated by our family, our reaction can affect how we eat, our behavior in personal and professional relationships and certainly our self-esteem.

Whether or not beautiful women really do get what they want, we've seen this idea communicated through all forms of media. Some of us have reacted to it by seeking forms of culturally subscribed beauty through dieting, taking pills, having plastic surgery, lying in the sun or on tanning beds, exercising, buying assorted products, anything, it seems, to be beautiful. Too often what we've bought is debt, disappointment and even entertained illness.

The emotional misery this imposed perception has caused is palpable. There are 10 million bulimics in this country, there are approximately $2 billion spent on cosmetics and $1.5 billion annually spent on diet plans. Clearly, if we feel deficient, it's good for the economy. On the other hand, some have conducted their lives in an opposite reaction to this legacy by becoming political and changing the perceptions of women and men in this culture. Also there are women in our country who have become angry, militant and have excluded themselves from intimate relationships because of their reaction to this transmitted boundary.

In this category, we must also include our reaction to parental expectations. Our perceptions of such expectations associated with gender, birth order, even historical era are all part of what the personality takes in. Parental reactions to raising a boy or girl, the eldest or youngest of the family, the historical era—flower children of the 1960s or a Depression era baby—become part of our boundary heritage.

Many of us conduct our lives in reaction to the boundaries that have been handed down to us. This style of reactivity is particularly prevalent in our personal and professional relationships. Some adults who were raised with abuse or abandonment react to childhood boundary patterns in ways that contaminate their lives and inevitably lead to a cycle of suffering. Their boundary patterns are established with others, not out of conscious choice, but in reaction to childhood trauma that was never metabolized. This is described thoughtfully by Alice Miller in her book, *Drama of the Gifted Child*, that describes adults who are imprisoned by recollections of abuse that affect all of their relationships.[1] For example, when intimate relationships become conflictual, our unresolved childhood pain can rise to the surface as rage, anxiety or shame. We may lash out, we may want to hide, we may become terrorized or become so anxious that we lie or talk incessantly. Our emotional and intellectual boundaries are so damaged that literally we don't know with whom we are interacting. Is it our father or husband? Is it our employer or critical mother? Is it live, or is it memory? Unfortunately there are too many relationships that are ruined by this kind of confused reactivity.

Louis was emotionally abused as a child by his father. He carries with him many of his father's injunctions: You'll never amount to anything, and everything you touch turns to garbage, and you're a spineless sissy. Louis has proved his father wrong by becoming an executive vice president of a large department store. Although financially he's successful, he has paid a high price. Unlike his father who was rarely employed and always home, Louis works such long hours that

---

1. Alice Miller, *Drama of the Gifted Child* (New York: Basic Books, 1994).

he rarely has contact with his family. When Louis' supervisor has the slightest criticism of his performance, Louis goes into a state of shame that is so severe, that he can't function and leaves work. His emotional reactivity to his supervisor has led to missed appointments and negative evaluations of his performance. During these episodes, Louis feels such a sense of failure that he returns home only to berate his own son and thus continues his father's legacy.

Professor Mary Main makes an important distinction between those (adults) who bear the negative burden of their childhood and those who have worked through it.[2] A critical task in recovery from any type of damaged functioning is learning how to discern positive and negative dimensions of reactive boundaries. In that discernment is choice.

3. Internalized Boundaries

Internalized boundaries constitute truly personal discoveries that may run counter to the mandates of culture, custom and family. This can happen whenever we decide to discover and set our own limits. These boundaries are formed out of intention and not based on reaction or anxiety-ridden defenses. Internalized boundaries can include some transmitted aspects from family or society, however they have been examined with discernment to fit the integrity of who we are and how we want to be treated. The process of developing internalized boundaries involves a physical, emotional and spiritual awakening that can alter the course of our lives. The development of internalized boundaries allows us to self-actualize and live with a sense of well-being. And of course,

2. Robert Karen, "Becoming Attached," *Atlantic Monthly,* Feb. 1990.

when we have a sense of ourselves, we are able to relate
effectively to others.

Family therapists such as Joseph Zinker and Sonia Nevis[3]
point out that internalized boundaries not only function as
outlines for individual identity, but also help to make sense of
complex relationships. As we develop more internalized and
healthy boundaries, we come to know who we are in relation
to others. We are aware that we have separate feelings, that
we think separate thoughts, that we enjoy a separate,
autonomous reality. Our spirit breathes free with the realization that no longer do we have to fear being swallowed or
overwhelmed by close relationships with others.

New Reasons for Being

The journey of personal healing is sometimes described as
a process of realignment, coming to that often unfamiliar
place of congruence where how we feel is clearly and directly
related to what we believe, and where our beliefs are consistent with how we act.

The gift of congruency is born out of courage, persistence
and commitment to self. All of these qualities are necessary
in order to make decisions that fit the rules, ethics and values
that enhance our integrity. We must become conscious of
what doesn't work for us any more and cease behaviors that
undermine our dignity. When we begin to internalize our
own boundaries, it's quite possible that those around us will
not be pleased. Inevitably we will need to take a stand by
saying things like,

"No, you may not treat me like that."

---

3. Joseph Zinker, *In Search of Good Form: Gestalt Therapy with Couples and Family*
(San Francisco: Jossey-Bass, 1994).

"I won't listen to this gossip."
"You're asking me inappropriate questions."
"I care deeply about you, but this is your problem to handle."
In an ideal world the people around us would celebrate our progress. However, when we change our agreements with others—how our relationship has always been conducted—if we expect them to celebrate our progress, probably we will be brought to despair. Some relationships will end as we grow, and in the long run we will attract people who honor our struggles and rejoice in our successes. Please remember to use the affirmation in the first chapter (page 17) to help you during those times that are frightening or difficult.

Dr. David Berenson tells a brilliant story that makes the distinction between those who actually leave the prison of entrapment and despair and those who keep redecorating their jail cells.[4] Yes, it is possible to keep decorating our jail cells with healing *concepts*, but we will never quite leave our cell until we put action to our desires. This never-ending challenge that we face all our lives is described by Dan Millman.

"No matter what we feel or know,
no matter what our potential gifts or talents,
only action brings them to life.
Those of us who think we understand concepts such as
commitment, courage and love,
one day discover that we only know when we act;
doing becomes understanding."[5]

---

4. David Berenson and E.W. Schrier, "Family Dynamics in Addressing Denial in the Therapy of Alcohol Problems," *Family Dynamics of Addiction Quarterly,* December 1991.

5. Dan Millman, *The Life You Were Born to Live* (Tiburon, California: H.J. Kramer Inc., 1993), 390.

READER/CUSTOMER CARE SURVEY

If you are enjoying this book, please help us serve you better and meet your changing needs by taking a few minutes to complete this survey. Please fold it and drop it in the mail.

As a special **"Thank You"** we'll send you news about new books and a valuable **Gift Certificate!**

PLEASE PRINT   C8C

NAME:_____

ADDRESS: _____

_____

TELEPHONE NUMBER: _____

FAX NUMBER: _____

E-MAIL: _____

WEBSITE: _____

(1) Gender: 1)_____Female 2)_____Male

(2) Age:
1)_____12 or under   5)_____30-39
2)_____13-15   6)_____40-49
3)_____16-19   7)_____50-59
4)_____20-29   8)_____60+

(3) Your Children's Age(s):
Check all that apply.
1)_____6 or Under   3)_____11-14
2)_____7-10   4)_____15-18

(7) Marital Status:
1)_____Married
2)_____Single
3)_____Divorced/Wid.

(8) Was this book
1)_____Purchased for yourself?
2)_____Received as a gift?

(9) How many books do you read a month?
1)_____1   3)_____3
2)_____2   4)_____4+

(10) How did you find out about this book?
Please check ONE.
1)_____Personal Recommendation
2)_____Store Display
3)_____TV/Radio Program
4)_____Bestseller List
5)_____Website
6)_____Advertisement/Article or Book Review
7)_____Catalog or mailing
8)_____Other_____

(11) What FIVE subject areas do you enjoy reading about most?
Rank: 1 (favorite) through 5 (least favorite)
A)_____ Self Development
B)_____ New Age/Alternative Healing
C)_____ Storytelling
D)_____Spirituality/Inspiration
E)_____ Family and Relationships
F)_____ Health and Nutrition
G)_____ Recovery
H)_____ Business/Professional
I)_____ Entertainment
J)_____ Teen Issues
K)_____Pets

(16) Where do you purchase most of your books?
Check the top TWO locations.
A)_____ General Bookstore
B)_____ Religious Bookstore
C)_____ Warehouse/Price Club
D)_____ Discount or Other Retail Store
E)_____ Website
F)_____ Book Club/Mail Order

(18) Did you enjoy the stories in this book?
1)_____Almost All
2)_____Few
3)_____Some

(19) What type of magazine do you SUBSCRIBE to?
Check up to FIVE subscription categories.
A)_____ General Inspiration
B)_____ Religious/Devotional
C)_____ Business/Professional
D)_____ World News/Current Events
E)_____ Entertainment
F)_____ Homemaking, Cooking, Crafts
G)_____ Women's Issues
H)_____ Other (please specify) _____

(24) Please indicate your income level
1)_____Student/Retired-fixed income
2)_____Under $25,000
3)_____$25,000-$50,000
4)_____$50,001-$75,000
5)_____$75,001-$100,000
6)_____Over $100,000

FOLD HERE

((25) Do you attend seminars?

1)_____Yes   2)_____No

(26) If you answered yes, what type?

Check all that apply.

1)_____Business/Financial

2)_____Motivational

3)_____Religious/Spiritual

4)_____Job-related

5)_____Family/Relationship issues

(31) Are you:

1) A Parent?_____

2) A Grandparent?_____

Additional comments you would like to make:

_____

_____

_____

_____

The Dance of Attachment and Kathy's Story

> *"To the degree that we are not held*
> *and bonded, we will find something to hold*
> *on to, some substitute for that holding*
> *that we did not get."*
>
> Sam Keen

The patterns of attachment we inherit and live out is the stuff of daytime or evening soap operas. Just watch Erica, the *femme fatale* who lures her victims with seductiveness but never lets anyone get too close. She's snide, manipulative, angry, and those around her want to keep her at a distance! Or there's Mary who goes through so many relationships in a month that it's amazing she has time to do her makeup! She's afraid of abandonment, anxious, insecure and becomes victimized after every commercial. I bet that Dr. John Bowlby and Dr. Mary Ainsworth, the creators of attachment theory, never dreamed that their work would give birth to such scholarly journals as the *Soap Opera Digest!* Although who knows, maybe they read romance novels between research breakthroughs.

Have you ever had the experience of trying to get close to someone who seems angry, aloof and appears to need no one? Or, have you ever known people who are so anxious and hypervigilant that no amount of reassurance or support will soothe them? What about that fellow at work who wants desperately to form friendships with others, but when the opportunity arises he just doesn't seem to know how to do it. If any of those scenarios sound like your own, then creating a state of comfort and well-being in a relationship probably sounds like a foreign concept. Those three examples are three primary patterns of attachment that were solidified by the time we were three years old! They were formed by the first relationships we had with our primary caregivers. These attachment styles are the original patterns from which we cut and design all of our relationships. But that isn't necessarily bad news, because there are methods to develop new styles once you know what your pattern is and how to change it.

While attachment isn't a dirty word, those in the addictions field, those who are struggling with dependent relationships, or those with a Buddhist orientation, might feel the word has a negative connotation. But I can tell you with some authority that you wouldn't be alive and reading this book if you didn't learn to attach to somebody in infancy! From the very beginning our styles of attachment not only influence individual development, but also shape future relationships.

University of Minnesota child development researchers Alan Sroufe and June Fleeson write that "early relationships forge one's expectations concerning one's self and others and they are the carriers of future relationships. One's orientation concerning others, one's expectations concerning their availability and responses, and what one can or cannot do to increase the likelihood of relationships are strongly shaped by our early attachments." [1]

---

1. Alan Sroufe and June Fleeson, "Attachment and the Construction of Relationships." Research paper, University of Minnesota, 1993, n.p.

Object relations theory tells us that the impressions that others make on us as children becomes imprinted into the still fresh "wax" of our psyches. As infants or toddlers, everything we feel is always in relation to others. If we're hungry it's because Mother isn't there feeding us. If we're happy it's because Father is there holding us. So, we see others as the source of the pleasure and the pain. Our whole sense of self is developed in relation to how others treat us, feed us and nurture us. Conversely, if parents are punishing and scolding, we develop different notions of who we are. So the way we attach to others is always based on our internalized representation of love objects in our lives.

The flexibility or rigidity of our boundaries, our ability to let in those who are safe and keep out those who are not, are greatly affected by the quality of our primary childhood relationships. Dr. Robert Karen, in an article that surveys the complex subject of becoming attached, says, "The infant needs to know that her primary caregiver is steady, dependable, there for her. Fortified with the knowledge of that availability, the child is able to go forth and explore the world. Lacking it, she is insecure, and exploratory behavior is stunted." [2]

Obviously this makes perfect sense, but we are unaware of how the nuances of these early attachment patterns impact our relationships.

All I Needed to Know About Relationships, I Learned Before Kindergarten!

Imagine that you are observing four children on a crisp October morning in a kindergarten classroom. Jack, Judy, Jill and Janice are playing with brightly colored blocks. Jack

---

2. Robert Karen, "Becoming Attached." *Atlantic Monthly,* February 1990.

seems to be not much interested in what the two little girls want to build. He has a small stash of blocks and is making a short tower at some distance from the main pile. From time to time, he glares at his companions as if to warn them to stay away. Except for that, his two playmates might just as well be in another room! Jill is enthusiastic but frequently agitated by the experience and is easily frustrated when things don't go her way. She cries or flares into a rage when she can't have the block she wants, or when the other two children decline to do her bidding. Janice starts to approach the girls but freezes and becomes awkward and withdraws into her own daydreams. Judy does not let Jack's aloof behavior or Jill's tantrums interfere with her fun. She involves them in her play as she can, amuses herself when she must, and asks the teacher for help in building a structure that will please and delight herself and her playmates.

If these children are blessed by wise and discerning teachers, they will all benefit and grow psychologically during their school years. Unfortunately, overcrowded schools and overburdened teachers mean that many educators react to children selectively. That is, whoever produces the least disturbance is thought of kindly. If children develop alienating strategies to face the world as they know it, they are bound to test the patience of adults and peers. The message they send to anyone who gets close enough to listen is: "People will never love me. I am an irritation." Unfortunately, the adults in their lives will react to their message with sometimes tragic consistency.

Children like Judy, who are cheerful and confident, most likely will be treated in an age-appropriate way and will be rewarded for their balanced conduct. However, early in their school lives emotionally insecure kids like Jill will be designated as one of the "problem children." Teachers will excuse her agitation whenever possible, but will become annoyed and impatient with her outbursts. Worse yet, some teachers will infantilize the clinging behavior of the Jills in their classrooms and these anxious children will either be treated as infants or warned to act their age. Distant children like Jack will be labeled sullen, angry or uncooperative, and many teachers will find themselves barely resisting the urge to shake them by the shoulders. Janice probably will be ignored, barely be noticed by teachers and counselors who are grateful that she's not causing any disruption. That is, until her adolescence when her longing for closeness may compel her to investigate drugs, gangs or sexual promiscuity.

These children are not just exhibiting inborn personality traits. Their attitude and interactions reflect the quality of bonding they received from their caregivers. Learning about primary patterns of bonding can provide us with the basic framework in understanding how we do the dance of relationship.

Judy was the beneficiary of *secure attachment*.[3] She received consistent, adequate attention from "good enough" parents who were products of a secure parenting environment.[4] Judy thus has become as wealthy as any heiress, with the precious legacy of psychological well-being. She has access to a clear set of boundaries that shapes her sense of self and helps her to determine what she needs from others. These boundaries will enhance her sense of well-being and allow her to form healthy relationships. It's important to point out that secure doesn't mean that Judy has perfect parents, there are no such creatures! Rather, she enjoys the gift of parents who are consistent and treat her in age-appropriate ways. Secure bonding has implications far beyond emotional well-being. Studies on

---

3. Mary Ainsworth, et al. *Patterns of Attachment* (Hillsdale, N.J.: Erlbaum, 1978).
4. D.W. Winnicott, *Talking to Parents* (Reading, Massachusetts: Addison-Wesley, 1994).

resiliency suggest that children who have histories of secure attachment with parents or other caring adults are more socially competent in school, both with their teachers and among their peers.

Jack, who avoids contact with other children, is an example of a child with an *avoidant attachment* history. This is a child who never received the consistent love and attention he needed and now tries to show the world he can get along without it. He was raised by parents who were needy, narcissistic, and couldn't tolerate displays of emotion. Like many children, Jack learned quickly what was and wasn't acceptable in his family. Because his responses weren't tolerated, Jack now holds people at a distance. Instead of setting boundaries, he builds walls and partitions that separate him from his true emotions.

Janice is a child who is uncertain how to connect to other children. She has lived in a foster home since she was two and has witnessed a violent murder. She doesn't know how to attach to another human being. She tries often to approach others but then freezes. She spaces out during school and is painfully shy and withdrawn. This is a classic example of a child with a *disorganized attachment* style, a pattern that occurs in children who have been hideously abused or neglected, usually before age five. Frank Putnam, an expert on dissociative disorders comments that these are the children who are more likely to form dissociative disorders and even multiple personalities in childhood.[5]

Jill is an extroverted child who enjoys play, until someone tries to leave or take control. She exhibits the effects of an *anxious attachment*. She is being raised by an alcoholic parent

---

5. Frank Putnam, *Diagnosis and Treatment of Multiple Personality Disorder* (New York: Guilford Press, 1989).

who comes through for her only once in a while and now she has an overwhelming hunger for caring and closeness. She has no boundaries when it comes to others because she can't tolerate separation. She learned manipulation early in her life, attempting to feel some control in a chaotic alcoholic home. Remember, intermittent reinforcement is what drives rats crazy! When a child receives intermittent love and attention, that child becomes wildly addicted to the behavior of his or her caregiver.

Under the category of anxious attachments, there is a pattern called a *traumatic bonding* which develops when a child is treated with loving attention followed by mistreatment or abuse. This causes a very strong attachment to the abuser. Like any addictive pattern it is replicated too easily. So, if teachers or counselors are using a calm and warm style followed immediately by confrontation, some individuals, like Jill, will go into a state of fear bordering on terror. Traumatic bonding is the context of relationship for many abused women. I believe that this addictive bond, combined with financial constraints, are the primary reasons that battered women stay in dangerous relationships. We must be conscious of childhood attachment patterns so we don't replicate them in adult relationships. Unless we're doing some form of psychodramatic work, the results are harmful and counter productive, particularly in the case of abused women and children.

The anecdote for insecure attachment patterns is to be treated differently. Sounds simple, doesn't it? Most of us would agree. However, it's challenging at best to respond with warmth and calmness to people who are clingy, anxious, withdrawn, angry and rejecting. As a "recovering" high school teacher, I know that my first response to kids who were acting out was probably the exact response they got from their parents! My response wasn't intentional, and that was the problem. If I paused before

I reacted, I may have been able to respond intentionally in ways that didn't reinforce these insidious patterns. I wasn't aware that treating kids differently could begin to heal the wounds of insecure attachment.

Most clinicians know that the relationship that develops between therapist and client is the healing factor. The following story illustrates how we cannot underestimate the power of empathy and connection in changing how we see ourselves and the world. Debra was a nine-year-old who was physically abused by her caregivers. She had lived in many foster homes by the time she was seven and developed an avoidant/disorganized attachment style. Her grandmother was suing for custody and Debra had to appear in court. My friend, a psychologist, decided to take on the job of getting her ready for her appearance.

When Debra first walked in the room, she stood in the corner and wouldn't get near me. I remember she couldn't get her zipper open and refused my help. When I approached her, she looked at me with a frown and told me to go away. It took two weeks before she could even look at my face! I worked with her several times a week for over two months, and during this time we started to establish a relationship. I read to her, occasionally we laughed together, and I knew she was beginning to trust me.

After ten weeks it was time for her to go to court and I knew I may not see her again. The last day, Debra came in the room and gave me a long hug. She had never done that before. I held her and told her that all of us want parents who love us more than anyone on earth. Sometimes we get parents who love us, and sometimes we get parents who hate us. I wanted her to know that I had come to love her and that I was the first in a long line of men and women who would give her that love, so she could start looking for us. Sometimes having others love us is just as good as having parents who love us. I knew I was one of the first loving women in her life and the quality of the connection between us would be remembered in her body and in her heart. And through that bond she may know that it's possible to have this kind of comfort within herself. She may even learn to embrace the idea of an unconditionally loving Spirit!

Whether our past was filled with pleasure or pain, this is the kind of loving connection that we all need. If we didn't get what we needed as children, it's not too late now to create comfort and safety.

From Generation to Generation

Attachment patterns are an issue that persists long after school is completed. While secure attachment enables children to develop healthy relationships as children and adults, ineffective or damaged attachment patterns in adulthood are also a result of childhood family relationships.

Our boundary patterns are intergenerational, so we're all born with responsibility for determining what pattern(s) was transmitted to us, how we react to it, and what boundaries we choose to internalize and make our own. Typically, whatever attachment model was developed will tend to remain, unless we do our work. As you read the vignettes earlier in this chapter you saw how the parents' style of attachment and their boundary issues manifested in their children. Since there is an intergenerational transmission of boundaries and attachment patterns it's crucial to break the cycle of suffering and violence so we don't pass it down to our own children.

Dr. Mary Main of the University of California at Berkeley, has dedicated her life's work to the research of these patterns that are passed down through the generations.[7] Her conclusions underscore the importance for all of us who are parents, teachers or have contact with children to do our work. According to Dr. Main, there is a strong correlation between how we *remember* and communicate about our relationships with parents and the quality of affectional bond that we will pass on to our children. There are three primary patterns that are transmitted through this process:

Autonomous Pattern

These are adults who remember their childhood experiences with their parents and have been able to incorporate painful memories into insights and wisdom. It's not that these people had perfect parents. On the contrary, some of these adults have histories of violence or neglect. The distinguishing factor is that they have become conscious of their childhood trauma and have been able to work through this trauma. These adults will tend to raise children who have healthy, secure attachment patterns.

Dismissive Pattern

There are those individuals who seem indifferent to their childhood relationships. When asked about their parents or their childhood experiences, they will often seem put off by the question! They may remember little or nothing, or offer idealized portraits of their parents and family life. However, if and when they start describing some of what they recall,

---

7. Robert Karen, "Becoming Attached." *Atlantic Monthly*, February 1990.

details of neglect, rejection or terrorizing emerge that contradict their portrait. Adults with this dismissive pattern will tend to raise children who develop an *avoidant* attachment style.

Preoccupied Pattern

There are some of us who can't talk about our childhood without being flooded with intense negative memories. We are confused about our relational past. Describing our childhood causes feelings of anger, anxiety and neediness. Typically, we define ourselves as adult children. We may be in the process of working through these memories or we may remain stuck in the past, continuing to blame our parents for all our troubles. Our children will tend to have an *anxious* attachment style.

Although as parents we have the best intentions for our children, without taking charge of our lives by becoming conscious of our childhood patterns and learning to transcend them, we will pass on the cycle of suffering. Many of us have left our families and have sworn that we will never recreate the kind of rigidity or chaos we were raised with. What we know is that history does repeat itself and it is well worth the effort to turn our painful childhood experiences into the kind of wisdom and insight that we can give to future generations. The following by George Bernard Shaw speaks about this legacy.

This is the true meaning of life:
To live for something recognized by ourselves as a
    mighty cause.
To be a force of nature,
Rather than a feverish little clod of grievances and

ailments, complaining that the world is not
devoting itself to making me happy.
Life is its own splendid justification.
I don't believe that life is a flickering candle,
I believe it is a splendid torch.
And I want to make it burn as bright as I can
Before I hand it down to my children . . .
    and future generations.

Kathy's Story:
A Few Affairs to Remember

Kathy is 33 years old, fit and trim, with alert, intelligent eyes and a striking mane of hair. She is athletic, fun to be with, style-conscious and rarely without a romantic relationship with a man.

Bewildered by successive failed relationships she has entered into psychotherapy. She's trying to face her assumption that she needs a man and a relationship in order to have any chance of feeling good about herself. "When I am with a lover," she confesses, "I know exactly who I am and what I want. He takes charge of everything. When we are finished, I can't even decide what to wear in the morning. I can still function at work, but I feel like a non-person the rest of the time."

For the last seven years, she has held a job as an administrative assistant in a large realty company. Her image is impeccably professional, and she is competent at her job, but she has built seniority on the fact that she has become indispensable to her male boss. His wife doesn't know that Kathy is the one who bought her Christmas, birthday and anniversary presents every year since 1987. Kathy is charming and a good conversationalist, but also adept at generating a smoke screen when she is told to do so. She is accustomed to running interference for her boss, so much so that customers and co-workers often experience her interaction as an artificial performance. That technique has seeped into her personal life. Even though she stays current with local and national events, her comments often seem shallow and devoid of genuine opinion or feeling. On another level, Kathy is unaware of the physical and emotional impact she has on others. Her physical appearance embodies many a man's fantasy, and she is both spontaneously affectionate and practiced at self-giving. But she has little idea how seductive she is, or how exciting and provocative her touch and willing manner can appear.

When Kathy was 17, she graduated from high school and immediately moved in with an older lover. She decided to shield her parents from that knowledge by renting her own apartment, without ever intending to live there. Eventually she married her lover and they stayed together for five years. Since then, she's had two relationships in succession, each lasting about five years. As if to convince herself of her own autonomy, she's retained the apartment all that time, even though she has only lived in it for a few weeks over 16 years.

Her tendency had been consistent to define herself against the template of her partner's opinions rather than to trust her own assessments. If her lover was angry at her, Kathy judged herself bad. If he was pleased, she felt worthwhile and good. After a magical evening with a lover, she'd look in the mirror and see a beautiful woman. If the evening went badly, she could see only ugliness and physical defects—nose too big, breasts too small, thighs ungainly. When he listened to her, she felt intelligent; when he didn't, she felt stupid.

Not only did she render herself totally dependent on his reactions, she avoided making close female friends who might have challenged her behavior. Her three serious relationships each ended when the man walked out, leaving her feeling abandoned, disoriented, sad and lost. In each case, she believed that her lover left because of her deficiency.

When her last love affair crashed, she compensated for the pain in her customary style. She bought a new wardrobe and some jewelry, had an expensive make-over, went out to the local hot spots where she began a number of casual but intense sexual episodes, each of which felt a lot like warmth and closeness at the time. The two most lasting benefits of this behavior, however, were debt and shame.

As she talks with her therapist about her family life it becomes clear that the damaged boundaries of childhood relationships have been carried into Kathy's adult relational patterns. The only child of an alcoholic, domineering mother and a passive, distracted father, Kathy never received adequate emotional support from either parent. Her mother controlled Kathy's every choice—clothes, friends, dictating just how close any of her relationships could be. Her father coped with his wife's addiction, and her anger over an accident that prevented her from having any more children, by closing off from his surroundings and refusing to entertain or express deep feeling.

Like surviving in snow or sun Kathy changed her clothes or behavior to survive in the only climate she knew. She deferred to her mother in every decision and secured irregular affection from her father by playing the little girl long after she had grown past that stage. As an adult she had no capacity to think for herself and she looked to others not only to solve her problems but also to provide her with a sense of identity. Further, she believed that the way to a man's heart was to remain a helpless child since this was the way she secured her father's occasional attention. Since neither of her parents admitted to their own problems, Kathy blamed herself as the cause of any family crises. When things went wrong in Kathy's adult relationships, she naturally assumed that the fault must be hers.

It will be a challenge in Kathy's therapy sessions to uncover a different system of belief about intimate relationships and about the value of her own identity. For too long she has been convinced that true love means losing herself in the identity of a man, surrendering totally to her male partner's opinions, expectations and will. Predictably, this is what has happened in her relationships, and it has left her devastated when love comes to a end.

Contrary to what Kathy learned in her family as a child, real intimacy is forged when two people are as honest as they can be about who they are and are present for each other in that honesty. It will take some time for Kathy to learn how her little girl self distorts her perception of adult men who enter her life and especially in terms of what it means to love one another with adult mutuality. When Kathy can take some time to discover who she is without a primary relationship, she will learn to contain the images and feelings that stem from her childhood.

CHAPTER 5

Boundary Violations and John's Story

"Each one of you is here on this
earth because you have something very
important to see in yourselves and struggle
against, with all your skill and ingenuity,
with all your strength of mind and
will and soul and heart."

Maurice Nicoll

There are reasons that we feel unable to protect ourselves physically, emotionally, intellectually and
even spiritually. Most of these factors have their
origins in the past. Since we must be aware of our
past before we can transcend it, I want to describe what happens in each category of boundaries that prevents us from
existing in comfort and safety.

Please keep in mind that we are much more than our
biographies. We are much more than abuse survivors, incest
survivors or adult children of clinically interesting families.
In time we come to know that some of the labels we use to
describe ourselves are limiting, and they can impede our
growth if we imagine they encompass all of who we are.

Before I begin this process, I must confess that I am a first
born child and I like structure. For that reason, my description of boundaries will be done systematically. However, the

truth is that boundaries exist simultaneously and are not particularly orderly. Physical, emotional, perceptual and spiritual boundaries are all intertwined. For example, if you berate me, I experience a *physical* reaction. On the other hand, if I am physically abused, I will be affected both *physically* and *emotionally*. Any form of abuse will alter the way I look at the world and certainly will give me pause before I embrace the notion about a loving power in the universe! One of my mentors taught me that *you have no rights unless you claim them*. Therefore, so you can claim yours, I will describe the four categories of boundaries, what keeps us from using them, and how each contributes to our identity, well-being and safety.

Physical Boundaries

Physical boundaries ensure that we can identify where we end and others begin, and can, therefore, protect ourselves against invasion by others. Just as important, they help us guard against intruding past others' physical boundaries. We can think of physical boundaries as a "skin screen" that serves to protect our physical selves and, indeed, our entire boundary system. It is often the first boundary that is violated, which then hampers our ability to develop healthy boundaries in other areas of our life.

Typically, boundaries are violated by *intrusion* or by *distancing*. Unfortunately, examples of physical intrusion are plentiful: from physical violence, incest, unwanted sexual attentions to unwanted tickling, patting or hugging. Distancing is common as well and involves neglect, withholding touch or affection and ignoring, among others. Even if there are no visible scars, the wounds of intrusion and distancing are vivid and insistently painful.

Ask a roomful of people to describe when their boundaries

were violated and responses will explode against your ears
like popcorn: I was robbed. I was molested. I was guilt-tripped
to death. She read my journal. I was intimidated, ignored,
beaten, cheated. He abandoned me. But few people think to
mention the more common violations that everyone has felt:
when they were interrupted in mid-sentence, when someone
entered their room without knocking, when someone
touched them too soon or too seductively.

Physical intrusions involve invasion into our body boundaries, that space that surrounds our physical selves.
Boundaries change with the passage of time. What is appropriate space in one generation may seem to be uncomfortably
close or impossibly distant in another. As late as the seven-
teenth century in England, duels were fought because someone brushed too close to another person on a public sidewalk!
In the 1960s and 1970s it seemed permissible to hug and
touch anyone within range. Today, if someone stands too
close to us in the automatic teller line outside the bank we
feel almost the same discomfort as if we were being touched.
Everyone's limit is different and varies according to time,
place, gender, even culture. But if we have no guidelines to
discern when our space is being violated, we may not be
aware when someone has been dangerously inappropriate.
Remember, we are the only experts on our own boundaries.

We can identify readily more dramatic invasions of physical boundaries, such as abuse, battering, incest, rape. A less
dramatic but equally significant invasion occurs when others
inappropriately satisfy their own needs for affection through
gratuitous or excessive hugging and holding. *Sexualized affection* by an adult toward a child is the foundation for later
confusion. This occurs when children can feel the sexual
energy, but they can't name it and aren't sure how to respond.
When a child shrinks from a kiss on the lips from a parent or
a tobacco-tinged nuzzle from Uncle Joe, probably it isn't from

shyness. Most likely the behavior disturbs them, but they don't know how to avoid or resist the affection of adults who are *supposed* to be loving. Children who are covertly abused in this way become confused about the boundaries between sex and affection. When these children become adults they may misconstrue messages of affection as flirtations. They may be drawn to people who send out mixed messages. And they may ignore danger signals that are cloaked in seductiveness, thus putting themselves in compromising if not dangerous situations.

Sometimes adults look back on childhood and remember incidents when they were held too closely by a pastor, a teacher or a sports coach. Even though the encounters may have been entirely innocent, their boundaries were violated and their physical limits were made more permeable or precarious. People often have experienced being bound tightly by a butterfly bandage or pierced by various probes and instruments, from an ice-cold stethoscope to an enema syringe. If that happens more frequently than medically necessary, being thus violated can cause development of passive personalities, which exposes them to easy victimization. In our culture it is hard to admit that procedures such as enemas or the use of a speculum are violating, because they have a medical aura about them. We live in a society where, if an authority figure says something is good for us, we accept it as gospel. If we can recognize that we are being violated, we can confront this kind of violation and protest.

Instead of forming too permeable or precarious boundaries, some of us compensate for an inadequate or non-existent physical limit caused by abuse or neglect by constructing walls. If, for example, touch has been dangerous and unpleasant, we may screen out all advances by non-verbal messages. Our body language, lack of eye contact and facial expression say, "Stay away. Don't come near me. I am not available for connection in any way!" Unfortunately, behind our wall hides a lonely, hurting, needy child who desperately wants connection, but is deathly afraid.

Jeannie, a shy, introspective college student, is carrying unacknowledged memories of years of sexual aggression from her uncle. She is a fiercely dedicated student. She studies constantly and arranges her books in the library to form a barrier around her portion of a common study table. She looks up and glares when others approach, as if defying them to penetrate the defenses of her refuge which are her books, her studies, her silence, and the expression of hostility on her face. Ironically Jeannie is *touch-starved*, but cannot let herself acknowledge the extent of her neediness. To her, touch means danger and her full-time job is to create an island of safety.

Conversely, when children are deprived of affection and touch it leaves them longing desperately for a source that will meet their needs. For example, a little girl who never received the affection she needed from a distant father became a receptionist in a major corporation. For reasons she cannot fathom, she tolerates it when her middle-aged boss gives her what he characterizes as a friendly hug goodnight, but then holds her a little too long and a little too tightly, and finally begins caressing her back. She endures his attentions because she is starved for affection, but it creates ambivalent feelings: the hug feels good but it generates intense feelings of shame. Desperately trying to hide her feelings of discomfort and dread, she returns to her apartment with an inexplicable sense of emptiness and defectiveness.

Most of us can comprehend and feel the limits of our physical boundaries. But for many who have been violated or even subtly had their physical boundaries permeated, it is a daunting task to repair those boundaries and stop unwanted touch or violations. Inevitably, *we treat ourselves the way we were treated*, because that's what we know. Therefore, boundary violations that happened to us that were forms of abuse, now cause us to continue to abuse ourselves in a variety of ways. For many of us it's a lifelong task to stop abusing our own bodies through addictions, by ignoring pain, or generally disregarding our health and well-being.

Emotional Boundaries

Of the four categories of boundaries, emotional limits are perhaps the most complicated. In general, emotional boundary blurring happens when the "container" that cradles our constellation of feelings is invaded or neglected by ourselves or by others. People whose emotional boundaries have been trampled on become either super-reactive or emotionally shut down. Some of us become walking mine fields where the wrong expression or gesture can trigger an explosion. Many of us know about becoming overreactive and sometimes abusive over seemingly benign events, *especially* in our intimate relationships. The catalyst for our reactivity can be anything from a compliment to someone's crying, a facial expression or even a burnt dinner.

David, a respected book critic for a major newspaper, was regularly beaten by his father, a self-made financier who resented David's expertise of the language. Today, David's comfort zone is intact at work where he spends long hours. His manners are impeccable at lectures and book signing events, but it's a family secret that he rages at his three-year-old son, Steve, when he cries too loudly and slaps his wife if she burns the dinner. Often he approaches home with a tight gut and a splitting headache that escalates when he walks in the front door. After these episodes David feels shameful and contrite and swears that *this* time will be the last outburst. But the truth is, he's out of control and cannot manage the rage that has been fermenting within him for 30 years. I wish there was a happily-ever-after to this story. Unfortunately, research shows that there's a predictable-ever-after and it's not particularly happy. Three-year-olds like David's son don't have the ability to metabolize a father's rage. Children of his age are astute observers, but lousy interpreters, and those who witness violent anger will assume that the anger is about them. As David continues to project rage and shame on his Steven, Steven will absorb those emotions. As Steven grows and enters into relationships, he will undoubtedly become pained and bewildered about the extent of rage or shame he feels, and projects, in turn, on his children. Healing will begin when he discovers that he is not only carrying his own anger, but the introjected emotions of his father. This is exactly how the legacy of violence, chaos and failed relationships gets passed on.

Along with deep shame and confusion, abused children feel a twisted sense of loyalty to their perpetrator. They grow to adulthood with the assumption that it is they who are defective and they sabotage themselves at every turn. Their efforts to develop physical or emotional boundaries are eroded by their inability to overcome this shame.[1] That's why it's important, indeed essential, for survivors of trauma to separate the abuse itself from the precious child who experienced it.[2]

When primary caregivers are in denial about their feelings or are irresponsible about how they express them, then those same feelings probably will be provoked in their children, particularly if the child is under five years. Because such a child cannot see that the source of these strong emotions lies outside

---

1. Marilyn Mason and Merle Fossom, *Facing Shame* (New York: Norton, 1986).
2. Renee Fredricksen, from a workshop on trauma and children in 1985.

himself, he will remain deeply perplexed and uncontrollably reactive. As an adult he may, as violated people usually do, shrug off his reactiveness and the consequences as simply "the way I am." Out of loyalty, children usually will take the blame rather than investigate their origins. Somehow, it's easier to suffer than to confront our parents' imperfection.

Young children have absolutely no boundaries against emotional invasions and few defenses against the withering aftershock of feelings and perceptions. When, for example, five-year-old Nikki sees his unemployed father fly into a rage, he thinks he's to blame and struggles to contain the intensity of his father's tantrum. It's like trying to contain an inferno of anger in a container designed to hold a small flame. Nikki doesn't know whose problem is whose! If his father would explain that his rage has nothing to do with Nikki, then this child would be spared the legacy of shame and rage that will haunt him for a lifetime.

How can we know if our emotional boundaries have been violated or damaged? When feelings are so continually overwhelming that they literally take away our breath or rob us of our will, it is a sign that our emotional tapestry may be contaminated with threads of unexpressed or reactive emotions of our parents or other authority figures. Natural feelings serve a purpose and usually don't overwhelm us. Emotions serve as radar to our inner and outer world. Enmeshed feelings, however, become like uninvited guests and overstay their welcome. Their signals don't provide us accurate information about the present. Rather, they are a carryover from the past, often based upon the perceptions of a scared child. When we are controlled by these emotions, we think and behave reactively. We are responding, not from who we are, but from what was bequeathed to us.

For example, Angie carried her mother's feelings. For years she had listened to her mother mourn the death of her husband. Frank had died when Angie was eight, and from the day of his funeral she had never had a chance to work through her own feelings about him. She never felt entitled to bear the sadness of a child who had suffered her own very real loss. Instead, she was the designated receptacle for her mother's feelings. As she grew older, she felt like a widow, never able to form or sustain a serious relationship because she carried both her own and her mother's grief.

To form an emotional comfort zone, it is imperative that we allow ourselves to discover what circumstances in the *present* trigger our reactions from the *past*. Think back over the week and try to remember what triggered you to became overreactive or numb. Was it a child who was out of control? Was it a particular person at work who rages? Was it a tone of voice that sounded too syrupy or phony? To take such an inventory, we must *slow down, take a deep breath,* and become acutely aware of what is going on outside of us, while scanning our inner world to note our emotional and physical reactions. These steps will let us see if the present event justifies our overpowering emotions, or possibly a paralysis that suppresses all our senses. This *slow down,* take a breath and be aware, is a dynamic that we will return to often as an important part of creating and healing our boundaries.

Remember, healthy emotions serve the purpose of keeping us sensitive to our interactions with our environment. Also, they help to call our attention to our behavior. Even though the following four emotions are often thought of as negative, they serve a positive purpose, unless they have become part of the legacy of damaged boundaries handed down through the generations.

Pain. Emotional pain can help us become aware of life's roadblocks. If something gets painful enough, it usually moves us to action. However, when our pain is joined to a parent's pain, we experience **hopelessness and depression.** Instead of becoming motivated to act, we find ourselves immobilized by despair.

Fear is a protective response intended to keep us aware of danger. It's hard to be aware if we inherited a strong dose of someone else's terror. Imagine a little girl who is deciding for the first time that she is going to cross the street. She has learned about traffic safety in school and looks both ways first for oncoming cars. As she is about to step off the curb, her mother sees her and screams out a shrill warning. "Don't you dare cross the street! You will scare me half to death!"

The little girl does learn *not* to cross the street but for what reason? Not to take care of herself, but to keep her mother from being afraid. As an adult she is unaware of the root of her own phobia when fear soars every time she's in traffic or on a crowded street. She thinks it is just part of the price of living in a big city.

Shame in small doses is one of the great motivators of human experience. German philosopher Friedrich Nietzche said that it is shame that "safeguards the spirit." It is an emotion that restores humility and reminds us that we're human. Shame prevents us from running to the grocery store naked. In other words, it can help us to form legitimate social boundaries. But when a parent uses shame to berate, belittle or humiliate, it becomes toxic to the health of a child. Imagine a young boy who is publically berated by his father for striking out in a Little League baseball game. The child feels shame. He has no way of knowing that father's tirade originates in a time when Dad failed to hit the ball and heard jeers from the crowd. Rather than helping him find the discipline he needs to be a good baseball player, his father is depleting the boy's store of confidence as effectively as one makes a cash withdrawal from an automatic bank teller. An overlay of parental shame diminishes the self with feelings of defectiveness.

Anger, the emotion that first helped us to push away from our parent's lap and assert our identity, is fanned into rage when combined with the anger of another person. When a young mother explodes hysterically at her two-year-old child in a supermarket, slapping his hand and berating him for having touched a piece of candy, something more is at work than a reprimand for a minor lapse in behavior. Why is she so overreactive? It may be fueled by generations of anger. Possibly the mother carries the anger of her husband, or is channeling her own rage at a father who abandoned her. Whatever the reason, the child will bear the brunt and store it in his own reservoir of misbegotten rage. Like a fire in a forest of dry trees, dysfunction perpetuates itself.

The impact of emotional violation can be global. It has been said that Hitler, raised by an abusive, raging father, deposited his deadly rage on millions of people because he had no offspring to feel the brunt of his wrath. While it is highly speculative to suggest that if Hitler had children there would have been no Holocaust, it is crucial to understand and discover the source of our emotional intensity, contain it, and begin the task of healing our emotional boundaries.

Intellectual-Perceptual Boundaries

A violation of intellectual-perceptual boundary can be elusive since the mind is built to rationalize its wounds. The violation occurs anytime someone tries to read our thoughts, pick our brains, or rape the privacy of our minds. Perhaps you have experienced someone's blunt attempt to "get into your head" and play dangerous games with your mind, wrapping their manipulative intent in sweetness, sarcasm, gossip or an assurance that you are special. If so, it is likely you know also the manipulative pull of blame, criticism or rudeness that tries to coerce your thoughts as surely as a slavemaster's whip. But for children who are in early cognitive stages, such subtleties are all but imperceptible. They see the world in black and white and have no internal filter to discern what is true and what is not. All too often parents' preoccupation with their own pain renders them insensitive to the impact their words have on children.

People who bully their point of view to center stage at the expense of other opinions and who discount other people in an obsessive desire to be deemed right, show no respect for the intellectual boundaries of those around them. Unrequested advice that is offered in the hopes of triggering our reservoir of guilt—you-ought-to statements, interruptions, voice-overs, ignoring of our ideas—all show little recognition of another's boundaries. And, when kids get little positive feedback upon the expression of their thoughts, they grow up with uncertainty and mistrust about their ability to think. If parents use ridicule, hurtful or unfair comparisons to deny a child's reality, or share inappropriate information to entangle their children in a web of dependency, they are wounding their children's minds in the process.

Teenagers are particularly vulnerable to this phenomenon. It is more than just attractive to follow the crowd when your intellectual boundaries are made fragile. Then the force becomes all but irresistible and it is impossible to "just say no."

Every despot, dictator or demagogue has recognized the power of fear, hunger, sheer desperation, to diminish people's capacity for intellectual discernment. Desperate people tend to surrender their reality to whomever seems to be in charge and embrace the ideas of any outlandish savior—a Bhagwan Rajneesh, a Jim Jones, a David Koresh—as if they were their own. Too many children seem doomed periodically to forsake their intellectual boundaries and follow a leader into tragedy or oblivion. If we had no other reason, this emphasizes the

critical need to reclaim the healthy boundaries that allow us
to trust and act on our own perceptions.

My public speaking experience furnished a graphic example of the perceptual damage we suffer as adults when our
reality is consistently invalidated. I was speaking to 150
adults, the majority of whom were from addicted families. I
was explaining the effects of trauma on children and was
mentioning five characteristics, of which number three was
Delusion—*refusing to believe that an event occurred despite all
the evidence to the contrary.* As I took a breath to continue, a
woman raised her hand and told me I had skipped point
number two. On the spur of the moment I decided to give the
audience a simple demonstration of delusion, and I declared
that I had not skipped it and prepared to go on with the lecture. The woman became upset and insisted that I had
skipped item number two. Again I claimed I had not and
asked her to look at someone's notes for the item so I could
continue.

The effect on the audience was palpable. A hush fell. No
one turned to the next person to check out their reality. It
dawned on me that I was in a roomful of adults who had surrendered their reality to me. Many sat with puzzled expressions on their faces, as if they were questioning their own
sanity. Finally, a young man asked me to please repeat item
two because he hadn't heard it.

I contrast this story to an example of a friend who has parented her daughter in ways she herself was not parented. It
was a stretch for her, but she validated her child's experience
of reality continually. One night, however, my friend's daughter awakened her during a thunder storm by pounding at the
bedroom door and saying how scared she was of the thunder.
Irritated, my friend said, "Mary, you are *not* scared. Go back
to bed!"

The daughter paused and then said, with the kind of

insight and courage that exemplifies a healthy intellectual boundary, "Oh really? Then what am I doing here!?"

There is no doubt that it takes work to monitor our intellectual boundaries, but it is the kind of work that eventually will allow us to relate honestly to others who would want to control what we believe and how we believe it. When we can develop an intellectual boundary, those who try to intimidate intellectually will have no bridge to cross into our minds and hearts.

The Old Fashioned Mind Scramble: Cognitive Dissonance

So often I have heard men and women tell with incredulous amazement about the fact that they couldn't see clearly what was going on in front of them. The statement I hear most is, "It was so obvious that he was that kind of person. Why couldn't I see it?" To understand this phenomenon, we must explore the origins of our patterns, including how we take in information. *That is, how we screen information through our perceptual-intellectual boundaries.*

Stories of men, women and children who have come to mistrust their own perceptions and rely on what others think have been written about in everything from romance magazines to ancient myths. A typical story is the "Emperor's New Clothes," about a sociopathic king who deludes the entire town into thinking he's wearing elegant robes, when actually he's wearing nothing at all. If we turn on any of the popular TV magazine programs like *20/20* or *A Current Affair*, or even the evening news, we see stories of people who are victims of fraud. Those stories are examples of the power of perceptual damage.

Research into the communication styles of families by Dr.

Paul Watzlavick and Dr. C. E. Weakland shows that a pattern known as *cognitive dissonance* occurs frequently.[3] When parents say one thing but do another, when others insist they know best about what we think or feel, we learn to distrust our perceptions of reality.

As a parent, I know it would be a great gift if we could teach our children to know what they see in front of them, with the surety of their whole being. As a therapist, I know it would be a supreme blessing if my clients would learn to trust their senses, their intuition and the information they are taking in from the outside world and the world beneath their skin. The hardest thing for adults to do is to unlearn patterns. Suppose Mom used to come home very drunk and violent, but insisted that you see her as loving? How about a father who used to pass out on the floor when he was drunk, but you learned to call it "Daddy's nap time." When all forms of bizarre events occurred at home and a child is told, "Nothing is wrong, go back to bed!" how can that child go out into the world and discern what is true and what is not? The fact is, the child cannot.

It's a frightening prospect to think of what happens to these kids and adults, who literally don't trust their own perceptions! They are dangerously vulnerable to peer pressure, gangs, gurus, religious zealots, seducers, embezzlers and anyone else who is strong and convincing. Therefore, if you've walked into the same hole in the ground too many times and came out bruised and in pain, don't be too hard on yourself. If you've asked yourself, "Why didn't I listen to myself, I had a huge knot in my stomach when I met this guy!" don't be too hard on yourself. You weren't trained to take in signals from

---

3. Paul Watzlavick and Charles E. Weakland, *Change: Principles of Problem Formation and Problem Resolution* (New York: Norton, 1974).

the outside and make decisions in your own best interest.

Consider the case of Brenda, who was told so often that her perception of what was going on around her was not reality at all that she learned to defer her perceptions to others. First, her father told that she didn't know what she was talking about. Then her teachers dismissed her questions as though she hadn't spoken. Then her boss tried to kiss her and when she protested said he hadn't done anything. Then her husband said that what she had *seen* and *heard* and *knew* to be a fact hadn't happened at all, that there was something wrong with her mind. Then her priest fondled and kissed her and denied that he'd done anything wrong. Reality for Brenda had become whatever the nearest authority person said it was, and especially if that person was male. Sad to say, but Brenda's case isn't unusual.

Please know that this is no small issue. On a larger scale, we need to acknowledge that presidents, kings, dictators and mass murderers have come to power with the support of people who cannot or will not see who these people are and what they are doing! Individuals who are so broken, desperate, hungry or lonely, that in order to establish some comfort and safety in their lives, they must surrender their reality to whoever is in charge.

So I feel bound to explain the dynamics that lead to this dissonance, in hopes that perhaps there are those who might make a decision to trust their senses. If there are parents reading this book, perhaps you will gain some insight that will help your children to fine tune their perceptions. Typically cognitive dissonance occurs in three different ways.

1. A child is punished by a parent or someone in authority for correct perception of the outside world.

    This happens with children when they are forced to perceive reality, not as it looks to them, but as someone else defines it for them. Mom and Dad have a screaming fight and break half the dishes in the kitchen. Suddenly they see their six-year-old standing terrified in the doorway. Dad says, "Don't worry, honey, Mom and Daddy were just having a discussion and these dishes just broke."

2. A child is expected to have feelings different from those she actually experiences.

   Eventually she will feel uncertain about anything she feels, unless she looks to someone else for approval. This is especially damaging to the process of identity formation which is so much a part of childhood, and so important in the conduct of adult relationships. People who surrender their feelings to significant others become invisible over time. Their partners feel for them, and speak of them in the third person, even when they are in the room. "Oh, Daddy really doesn't care about whether his brother visits at Christmas or not. He has got better things to think about. So do you! You should be happy. It is Christmas! Stop crying. Everything is fine."

3. If parents impose emphatic rules that both demand *and* prohibit certain actions, then the child is placed in a double bind where she can obey only by disobeying. For example, "Always be honest, *but* win by any means you can." or "Sex is ugly, *but* it is important to be popular with the boys."

   It is hardly surprising that people from such families can believe one way, feel something quite different, and act in ways that are incongruent with both. In the face of such deep contradictions, children grow into adults who learn to ignore their own wisdom and perceptions and literally are not willing to trust their own radar. The tragedy is that so many of us learn to surrender our capacity to discover and develop healthy behavior patterns.

Personal growth is a complex phenomenon demanding awareness of present day patterns and the childhood sources of those dynamics. Many of us have become aware of how our childhood patterns have damaged our adult relationships. But the more difficult task is to understand exactly *how* those patterns have affected us and then how to repair the damaged boundaries that resulted. Even more difficult is the sorting that must be done to see how each kind of boundary—physical, emotional, intellectual and spiritual—was affected and how to mature in that area.

Spiritual Boundaries

Spirituality is a sense that we are more than our feelings, our thoughts and our bodies, that we travel on this planet as spiritual beings in human form to experience the lessons of earth. Anything that interferes with our ability to become the kind of people we were meant to become by our Creator, anything that interferes with our knowing that we are lovable children of God, anything that destroys our striving to define the meaning of our existence can be considered a spiritual boundary violation.

Our attempt at spiritual definition is a paradox, since, in spite of formalized religion, no one can define spirituality for others. We each develop our personal definition of spirit throughout our lives, gathering evidence and ideas as we go, and often it's quite different from that of our teachers, parents, mentors and friends. This independence is necessary and yet it makes people with control issues uncomfortable. Indeed, history is filled with violent consequences for those who disagreed with or diverged from the doctrine which they were taught.

Spiritual boundaries are extremely vulnerable to violation. They are, as the Alcoholics Anonymous saying goes, "the first thing to go and the last to return." Yet they contain essential elements through which we build confidence about ourselves, our purpose in this world, and our relationship to the Divine within us. The seeds of spirituality are planted very early in life. From the day they are born, children learn to place their trust in unseen figures. Children are dynamically spiritual creatures. Their questions reveal curiosity about the rhythms of the universe. "Where does the night go?" "Is my hamster still happy even though he died?" They yearn to receive signs from adults that life is good, meaningful, ordered. This is why conclusions a three- or four-year-old reach about how good or bad the world is, determines the view of the world they may hold for the rest of their lives.

Often children derive their earliest ideas about God by observing their own parents. Through our parenting, we teach about God. If parents are angry, abusive or unforgiving or absent, childrens' feelings about God will be terror and uncertainty. Family dynamics have spiritual consequences. Child abuse engenders spiritual despair. An abused child feels abandoned by God and believes that there is no one to rescue her, in heaven or on Earth. Enmeshed family systems that force children to live out a parent's script for their lives, drown childrens' sense of spirituality because they must surrender any sense of their own path. If children are surrounded by people who have had more pain than blessings, they come to experience the suffering of the world much too soon. A child who is obliged to carry shame for an adult's behavior will feel a kind of spiritual bitterness that eats away at faith. "I must have been bad," the child thinks, "otherwise God would have done something to help me."

The type of discipline that parents use on their children can lead unintentionally to a spiritual bitterness. We might draw an example from a suburban backyard where little

Jimmy is building a frame for a tree house. He is not fully at home with tools and hits his thumb with a hammer as he tries to drive a tenpenny nail. He swears, in a voice loud enough to turn his mother's head. She doesn't see that his thumbnail is turning blue or that he is in pain. "Don't say such things, Jimmy, or God will strike you dead!"

For some, God never becomes anything other than an instrument of punishment. Twenty-two-year-old Jenny came home late from a date, her face streaked with tears. She could have been home by ten o'clock, but she had been walking the streets for the past three hours, avoiding home. On her date with her fiance she had sex and she didn't know how to hide from her parents what must be written all over her. She knows her parents would see her choice to have sex as they did all extramarital sex, as evil and unforgivable. They had convinced Jenny that their position was God's as well. "God sees all things and so do my parents," Jenny thought. "How can I avoid the punishment I deserve for my sin?"

How can we form any bond with a higher power or believe that God loves us unconditionally when there are those who convince us that God's whole job is to hold us accountable for our failings? Some parents are fond of playing St. Mom and St. Dad, which is another form of spiritual condescension. Saints also have disconcerting way of imagining that they are martyrs and demanding your veneration. When you are hurt and need a hug, they quote a Scripture.

With alarming regularity religious leaders lose sight of the fact that they are human, too, and use their power in inappropriate ways. When a priest wants a little girl to touch him in the name of God, no veneer of piety is thick enough to disguise the fact that an abusive crime is taking place.

I have observed that many sexually abusing families are fundamentally religious. When children go to church or synagogue and are told to forgive and forget, their ability to form any comfort zone, any sacred space in which to develop their spirituality is destroyed. When dad is abusing you, it does you little good to "just pray" that it will pass. It is important to forgive, but first children must forgive the world for letting this happen to them. Children need a chance to grieve a profound betrayal. Simply to forgive and forget is part and parcel of an offender-oriented society.

True spirituality is not a tool for denial. As with all the life-giving principles that shape our lives, we must come to own our ideas of Spirit for ourselves. This is done by forming a sacred space that moves with us at all times, to work, to our relationships and into the world. When we are ready to resolve the pain of damaged boundaries, then we form more loving, expansive images in which to embrace our emotions, our thoughts and our spirit.

Inherited Anger: The Next Generation
John's Story

This is a true story of a child whose emotional boundaries were damaged by the blunt blade of another's rage. John was an early baby boomer. When he was born his father was away fighting in the Pacific in the last days of World War II. John was his mother's center of attention, as well as his grandparents, his father's brothers, relatives from far and wide. He was never deprived of touch, of the soft croon of lullaby, of tasty food. When his father returned from the war, John's affection-rich environment shrank a little, but everyone remained close enough to look in on him regularly and let him know how much he was loved.

As he grew John became aware of how much his family resembled the ideal TV families of the 1950s, the Cleavers, Ozzie and Harriet with their universe of raglan sweaters,

Robert Young's predictable brood on *Father Knows Best,* sunny Donna Reed and her equally bright charges. John's dad was mysteriously employed while his mother was dependably at home. Neither of his parents drank or smoked and the family gathered regularly to read the Bible and pray.

But there was a weed in his paradise in the form of rage. His mother threw monumental tantrums that frightened him and his sister, and that his father weathered in cowed silence. There were times when his mother was a happy homemaker tending her children's needs. But when she couldn't bend the family to her will, she would launch into a screaming tirade about how she was an unappreciated household drudge, a victim of her family's demands who was going to get even by leaving them all flat. No response was allowed. When her raging was done she ran to the bedroom and slammed the door. After a while Dad went into the bedroom quietly and they could be heard talking. Eventually Mother would emerge, spent and mollified, unaware of the terrifying damage she had done.

John began throwing tantrums from preschool and all through high school. Because he was extraordinarily bright, teachers tolerated his towering rages but shared their alarm with his mother who was an essential member of the school PTA. She minimized the problem, "It's the way we are. We don't keep anything inside. We blow up at each other, but once it is over we are free of whatever is bothering us. John will learn to control his temper. It's just a phase."

The phase persisted. John moved from being a problem child to an angry young man. He vacillated from being dependent and needy to violently angry. He inflicted outbursts of rage on his own wife and children over inconsequential things like being stuck in the snow, not finding a parking place, a rebellious remark, towels on the floor of his daughter's room. His anger spilled over supervisors at work and he lost several jobs because he couldn't control his rage. Eventually, he threw himself with pious desperation into the work of the church where he hoped that God would reward his piety with peace of mind.

John exemplified an adult who had internalized his mother's violent anger and an anxious attachment style. Probably, if we were to investigate his mother's history, we'd discover that she too was enmeshed in a parent's pain that had been denied or irresponsibly expressed. Thus does the invisible but painful legacy of boundary violations move down a generational chain.

As a child, John believed that somehow he was responsible for his own anger as well as his mother's unresolved rage. Healing came for him because he took a deep breath and initiated an honest yet painful dialogue with his mother. His own shame had led him to delve into the source of his pain and risk rejection or even abandonment possible from his mother's denial.

So it was that at the age of 42 he talked with his mother late one night and urged her to explore her secret, that she was furious to have been consigned to adult life when she married at age of 19. She had been the youngest child of five, and suddenly she was expected to forsake that idyllic existence to accept a life of constant responsibility. Since John had married at 20 he had some understanding of how she had felt.

In the hours of that night, he risked suggesting that it was not just his anger that he had been carrying all those years, but his mother's deep resentment for sacrificing her youth too soon. Because she never talked about her rage and never claimed it as her own, John became enmeshed in his mother's rage and resentment.

As they talked, John began to feel as if a flood were subsiding in him. It felt like the release of overwhelming anger that he had carried for years. John was preparing to discover the threshold of his own anger rather than the overlay of his mother's rage which clothed the core of his identity. Now his healing could begin. He could begin to create a state of emotional well-being grounded in his reality, not his mother's. He could finally act on his suppressed instinct to push away from his stifling family closeness, and to experience autonomy clearly for the first time. In the internalization of his emotional boundary lay the serenity that had eluded him for years. It's true that wisdom comes, "wither through loving or suffering," and in risking both he discovered a chance to grow in self awareness and authenticity.

CHAPTER

6

All or Nothing at All: The Dynamics of Intrusion and Distancing

*"If our internal pendulum swings to one side,
it will inevitably swing to the other."*

Dan Millman

hen I was conducting group therapy, I used to marvel how consistently individuals who craved closeness moved toward people who demanded
distance. It's almost as if they scanned the room for
someone to connect to, until an internal homing device
announced, "This one isn't available for closeness, go for it!"

Tina, a woman in my group, constantly intruded on other
women's space, looking for attention and touch. She was
oblivious to their non-verbal warnings and charged right
ahead into their physical and emotional space. Of course the
women she chose were boundary distancers who either told
her harshly to back off, or resentfully acquiesced to her
needs. It was like watching a needy puppy try to cuddle with
a fire hydrant. It was painful to watch. All the women in this
group were experiencing pain in their relationships, and
their styles of intrusion and distancing were being played out

in front of me. Most of them were puzzled at the fact that they could have fallen in love with individuals who smothered them to death or wouldn't even touch them! Of course, that wasn't how their romances started, but it was the pattern that evolved.

Has there ever been a time in your life when you had great difficulty relating to male friends, male authority figures or lovers? Or, do you enjoy or even crave the attention of men and have difficulty with female friendships? If we can think back to our primary patterns of attachment, we will get some major clues why this is so.

Our boundaries are violated in one of two ways: one is by intrusion (invasive action) and another is by distancing (evasive action). Some of us were raised by parents who were intrusive, who craved closeness because they hadn't the quality of bonding they needed with their own caregivers, so they turned to their children. Some of us were raised by boundary distancers, parents who couldn't allow themselves to get emotionally or physically close to us. Probably the majority of us had combinations of both. Please keep in mind that I'm not talking about a normal balance between extroversion and introversion, but about families without balance so the styles are exaggerated and sometimes devastating.

Suppose a mother is physically or psychologically intrusive with her son. She intrudes his boundaries by searching his drawers, eavesdropping on his phone calls, confides information concerning her dissatisfaction with her marriage or holds him too tightly or too seductively. If this happens without intervention, likely he will become an emotional and physical *distancer* in relationships with women. This child may have problems with female friendships, lovers, even with supervisors or other female authority figures. He probably won't initiate relationships, but only react to a woman's assertive movement towards him.

The outcome of this process is gender determined and parents with several children will typically treat each child differently. So a daughter with a boundary intrusive mother will also have difficulty with female friendships and will distance herself from female co-workers, teachers and supervisors. If father is the intrusive parent, then she will develop a distancing style with men. The following is an example of how this boundary intrusion plays out in relationships.

Marianne is a college sophomore and really does want a boyfriend. She feels a bit out of place in her sorority to be one of the few girls who isn't dating. It's not that boys aren't attracted to her. On the contrary, boys have approached her often. However, after about three dates when romantic, physical contact is anticipated and some of the young men are ready to be closer, Marianne feels overwhelmed and starts to distance from the relationship. She isn't sure why she feels so suffocated. She just knows that when men start to become physically intimate, she feels like she wants to run away. What puzzles Marianne is that as the relationship gets more intense, she comes home from dates and remembers little about what occurred. While other girls sit up after hot dates and compare notes, Marianne gropes to remember the details and often has nothing much to say.

Marianne has seen a therapist and has ruled out sexual or physical abuse. She explained to her therapist that her father and mother are very loving and supportive. Her father, particularly, is so caring that he calls almost every day to check on how she's doing. In fact, her father's attention is something that he gives only to Marianne and not to her younger sister.

In therapy Marianne was asked to describe how she felt about her father's attention and exactly what kind of attention he gave her. Since she couldn't describe exactly what her father did, the therapist suggested that she call her sister. In a very painful conversation, her sister reminded her how intrusive her father was with her and how blatantly distant he was with her sister. When Marianne and her father were together, Dad insisted that she sit on his lap and cuddle. At 20, Marianne felt uncomfortable, yet reluctant to hurt her father's feelings. From the time she was very young, her father cuddled with her in bed and told her his problems, some of which were marital. When he phoned her each day, he insisted on knowing how she was feeling, what she was thinking and even what she wore that day. Her father bought her clothes and often sent extra money and made it known how special he felt when Marianne wore the clothes he picked out for her. Even though the conversations were uncomfortable, she allowed her boundaries to be violated again and again because she didn't understand what was happening. She loved her father, but she dreaded his visits and his phone calls. It became clear that the way she tolerated these constant intrusions was to space out. The minute she heard her father's voice, she would dissociate. It was no wonder she couldn't remember the details of their relationship!

An invasive parent creates in a child a sense that everyone who tries to get close will steal their very soul. If children spend their energy protecting themselves from abusive or invasive caregivers, they will have learned how to defend against others out of fear and anger. As adults they will protect themselves with walls that may take the form of passive-aggressive behavior or isolation. They may unconsciously lure others with the potential of warmth and closeness, but their fortress will be impenetrable. Finally, they will avoid the normal movement of deepening relationships because they sense their very existence is at risk!

It was important for Marianne to discover her primary pattern of bonding with her father to get to the root of her painful intimacy issues with men. Obviously, the discovery of this pattern didn't heal Marianne's relationships with men. But it's healing for her to know that she is not crazy, that her style with men is born out of woundedness and reactivity to her father's intrusive behavior. It's also crucial for her to realize how she dissociates when she feels overwhelmed. Her task is to claim the power of her boundaries, but first she must know what her limits are. It is virtually impossible to know your limits when you are dissociating. So the first step is for her to become embodied, to breathe, to learn some skills that she can use when she feels herself dissociating. It will be important to continue working with someone with whom she feels safe. Developing boundaries within a safe container is crucial.

Physical and psychological *distancing* also produce patterns in relationships that are puzzling and painful. When children can't get emotionally or physically close enough to parents, the children are forced to leave their comfort zones to chase after distancing parents. Again, depending on the gender of the child and parent involved, some patterns in adulthood may be predictable. When we analyze what we had to do to gain the attention and love we needed as children, it engenders sadness and anger. If a son can't get close to his mother, he'll become accustomed to leaving his comfort zone to chase that evasive parent. He may spend much of his adult life trying to compensate by attempting to fuse his emotional being to another through a series of intense and invasive relationships. Chasing after connection can take the form of manipulation, seduction, control and aggression. Of course, children who were raised with distancing parents will likely become boundary *intruders* with others of the same gender as their distancing parent. Jon's story describes this painful dilemma.

Jon is often in a relationship crisis. He says he just wants someone to share with, to touch, to hold and to cherish, and he doesn't think that's a lot to ask. When I asked him about

his early affectional bonds, he described a peculiar connection with his mother. To an observer Jon's mother probably
appeared to have given enough touching. She carried Jon
around with her, hung on her hip as she did her chores, or
when he sat beside her, she spoke to him and patted his back,
but emotionally she was absent. If he wanted loving or
focused attention from his mother, he had to scream. Then
finally she'd begrudge him attention. However, most of the
time Jon felt as if he were talking to an emotionally vacant
object. Sometimes she'd ask Jon to sit close to her in the car,
or while they were watching television she put her arm
around him and caressed him. However, Jon felt that their
relationship was emotionally empty.

As he grew up, his relationships with women never lasted
more than a few months. After a couple of dates, Jon wanted
to share his deepest, most personal experiences, he wanted
his date's undivided attention, he wanted to know everything
about "his woman." He smothered a prospective partner with
flowers, candy and even trips after only a couple of weeks.
However, there were always strings attached. His possessive-
ness and insistence on information was often too much for
them to handle. He couldn't understand why inevitably
women rejected him. Unfortunately, he was oblivious to the
cues women gave him until it was too late. He was so wounded
narcissistically that he assumed that women were crazy about
him and couldn't resist him.

Curiously, Jon was more interested in emotional connection than physical connection. He preferred cuddling to
making love and wouldn't initiate sex. If women were too
sexually assertive, Jon would back away. It's not that he didn't
enjoy sex with women and he truly was confused about his
lack of responsiveness. He questioned his sexuality until he
realized that the issue was one of boundaries.

If a primary caregiver is *physically invasive* but *emotionally distant,* the contrast produces boundary confusion like Jon's that causes mirrored, contradictory behavior, physically distant but emotionally intrusive. For instance, because of Jon's primary pattern of bonding with his mother, he tends to be emotionally invasive with women, but physically distancing. As children, none of us were able to prevent the inappropriate behavior or emotional abuse and neglect that parents inflicted. That much is obvious. What isn't so obvious is the emotional, psychological, spiritual or intellectual baggage that resulted that now affects our adult relationships. The following suggestions are for those who identify with either the invasive or the distancing pattern. Remember, no one can do this work for you. We must each recognize our patterns and then accept the job of healing ourselves.

Suggestions for Boundary Intruders

1. Learn to notice your feelings of hurt and anxiety that precede your desire to intrude someone else's space.

2. Learn to manage your anxiety by meditation, relaxation, exercise, getting support from friends.

3. Start with your family and set limits with them when necessary.

4. When fear of abandonment begins, be aware of when you leave your comfort zone. Learn to gauge this by tuning into your breath, your abdomen, your temperature and the intensity of your resentment or terror. If you're holding your breath or hyperventilating, if your gut is tight or you have stomach pain or diarrhea, if your face is getting hot or your hands are turning cold, if you feel your anxiety when you take a deep breath, then you need to take time out. Pull back and respond in ways

that are congruent with the wisdom of your body.

5. Notice the non-verbal cues of others and notice what happens to others when you come too close.

6. If you're in doubt about others' cues when you move toward them, you can ask the person you're with or get feedback from someone who is safe.

7. We must all face a spiritual void sometime in our lives. When we approach this emptiness, sometimes we charge ahead into another's space to counter our terrifying loneliness. When this emptiness occurs, it's helpful to seek out a spiritual advisor who can provide guidance and comfort. The longer we avoid the void, the more desperately we will turn to others who we think can fill our emptiness.

Suggestions for Boundary Distancers

1. Learn to pay attention to your fear and anxiety.

2. Get feedback from a friend, therapist or sponsor to see if your feelings of anxiety or fear are merited. Know that these emotions could be distorted and have their origins in past wounding.

3. Practice this affirmation: *I am willing to claim the power of my boundary. I can also make decisions to take small risks and know that I am safe.*

4. Learn to comment on your emotions as they happen. For example you can say, "I feel really anxious when you ask that question." Or, "I'm feeling overwhelmed, so I need time alone right now."

5. Practice setting limits for yourself that are congruent with how you feel. For example, you may not want to spend the night with someone when you are in a state of terror about whether or not you are safe.

6. Practice taking small risks with those you care

about: "I can't spend the night with you tonight, but how about going out for coffee and talking?"

Even though the invasive/evasive dynamic is complex, it's worth taking time to sort it out for yourself. With either dynamic we will display the self-destructive behavior that has kept us starved for intimacy from the very beginning. Often we get caught in cycles of denial around this dimension of relationship and it will take persistence to follow through on the insights that emerge. But you will develop a much clearer sense of your boundaries in the process!

Rules, Regulations and Consciousness: Creating a Sacred Reality

Would you spend money to build your dream home and then decorate it with old family furniture that you detest? Would you purposely furnish your office with desks and chairs that were too big for you? Certainly not! you say? Then consider this: Why would you create a life with rules that don't provide you with the safety and comfort that enhance your integrity and sense of self? It's ironic that we invest time and money creating an outer environment that fits our needs, when our inner world is out of sync. The rules and patterns we inherit give us the edge to achieve or the destiny to be miserable. Most of us have little or no idea of what rules we carry into adulthood that breed malaise and despair.

The following anecdote illustrates what happens in many families when adolescents are given rules they can't live by. This isn't about parent bashing. I have deep compassion for parents with adolescents. Coping with adolescents calls for great creativity. Did you know that the inventor of Valium was inspired by his 13-year-old son who used to steal his father's clothes to sell at school?

Several years ago an angry 16-year-old girl was referred to me by her school counselor for stealing, and her mother brought her in. Her mother sat in front of me wringing her hands furiously in a valiant effort to keep from wringing her daughter's neck. When I spoke to the mother, I found out that the family had so many rules that it was impossible to sneeze without being disciplined. It also sounded as if her daughter, Carrie, had been grounded since her tenth birthday. When Carrie finally spoke to me she indicated that she couldn't stand being at home and she listed some of the reasons: she couldn't talk on the phone after 7 P.M. she wasn't allowed ever to raise her voice or show anger, and she wasn't allowed to see her best friend because her father thought this friend wasn't a good influence. These rules were not subject to change or negotiation.

After meeting with the family for two sessions, it was clear that there were two underlying rules that governed the entire household. First, there was never a good reason not to be home. Second, it was disloyal to have friends outside the home that were more important to you then the family. Now, if by 16 an adolescent doesn't have friends who are more important than the family, he or she will spend a lifetime reacting to the rigid boundary the second rule dictates, unable to defy the gravitational pull of the family system.

I asked the distraught parents how Carrie disobeyed these two rules and a story unfolded that is one I've never forgotten. Apparently, one weekend evening Carrie was desperate to get out of the house. She found out that there was a choir concert at school and asked her mother if she could attend. Her mother said no, and gave no reason to justify her decision. Since getting angry was forbidden, Carrie knew she would be sentenced to another week of grounding if she expressed her anger. However, Carrie kept a journal and had discovered earlier that her mother read her journal. (I know it's a hideous violation, but what a way to get to her mother!) That night, Carrie took her journal and wrote a paragraph about how hard it was to be gay at 16, and left the journal where her mother could see it.

The next day when Carrie got home from school, her mother, father and the minister were waiting for her. Her mother had swollen red eyes but couldn't say why since she was not supposed to read the journal in the first place!

I appreciate that for those who struggled with their sexual identity at 16, this isn't particularly funny, and I don't condone Carrie's trickery, but it was the only escape she could think of in light of the no negotiate, no anger rules. Her parents were unaware that their rules caused more pain than comfort, since they both had been raised in homes that were chaotic, and they established family boundaries based on their reaction to those rules. Since it's a teen's task to separate as part of his or her individuation process, and if there are rules that prohibit this separation, it will obstruct severely their ability to have healthy relationships in the future. Today Carrie is 20, living in Europe and is a flight attendant. She travels all over the world and can't sustain a relationship because she's never home. What a surprise!

There's no factor more important to our comfort and well-being than the rules we inherit and live by. Rules are even more powerful when you understand that they have been constructed and determined over generations in the family. They are passed on as surely as we pass on our genes and they are just as powerful in their ability to shape our boundaries, personality and expectations. In healthy families, rules are used to *guide*, to *instruct* and to *protect* children. There can be a sense of safety and security within the family when children know the rules and the appropriate consequences for breaking those rules. This is particularly true when rules can be negotiated as children get older, and consequences are handled with consistency, firmness and gentleness.

As in Carrie's family, sometimes rules are so rigid that kids can only succumb or rebel. Parents may mean well, but the rules they establish don't serve the purpose of instruction, guidance or protection. Instead, some family rules are so ambiguous that no one knows what roles and tasks are assigned to whom. Those raised in rigid or ambiguous environments are all too aware that rules are used to punish, limit and restrict and the consequences for breaking these rules are inconsistent, violent or nonexistent.

One quality that helps to maintain our well-being is being able to work through problems from beginning to end. When rules are ambiguous or rigid, it's hard for families to work through crises. Either problems are denied or kept secret and discussion is discouraged. Like walking in a mine field, children are rarely certain when a bomb will explode or when some loose wire will trigger a reaction.

Lets say that Dad comes home and says that he's lost his job. In a healthy family, he might call the kids together and announce that he lost his job and perhaps explain why it happened. He might say that the family has to cut back on expenses for awhile, and he is working with an agency that will help him find employment. Contrast this with the environment of confusion or control. If Dad loses his job, children find out indirectly and how or why it happened isn't explained. If he finds a job, it appears to be an act of fate. Since children never witness the process of working through a problem from beginning to end, there remains a pervasive mystery about their own process. As a result there are millions of adults who live in a perpetual state of discomfort and insecurity. When life problems arise they aren't equipped with the skill to solve their problems and have little awareness of how they got into the mess in the first place. They may be successful professionally, but don't even understand how that happened, to the point where they feel as if their success must be a mistake!

I have worked with many adults who have inherited their families' confusion, and literally leave home in a perpetual fog. One young man I worked with was a medical student who had worked terrifically hard to get into medical school. He felt like an impostor and was certain that his acceptance must have been a computer error. His belief influenced his progress in school and he felt unsuitable to be a doctor. He dismissed his long hours of studying and all the social activities that he sacrificed to make good grades. In the course of his therapy I assigned the task of interviewing friends and teachers, and then outline the activities that led to his acceptance into medical school. For anyone who devalues their progress or is uncertain about how or why they are successful, this may be a crucial process.

Dr. Salvador Minuchin studied the dynamics in which families form their boundaries, and coined the terms *enmeshed* and *disengaged*.[1] Neither enmeshment nor disengagement are necessarily pathological styles of relating. Both styles are passed down by a system of rules within the family that dictate how relationships are to be conducted. For example, in healthy enmeshed families parents are easily accessible and there is a sense of empathy and warmth that pervades the household. Healthy disengaged families have consistent, very clear rules. There is love and affection, but rules that dictate when that love and affection are available. In these

---

1. Salvador Minuchin, *Families and Family Therapy* (Cambridge, Massachusetts: Harvard University Press, 1974).

families independence is fostered and children learn to face the consequences of their behavior. Unfortunately, either dynamic can become detrimental if parents are unconscious about their reactions to their own relational past.

Enmeshment becomes pathological when we have to sacrifice our individuality to receive love. When boundaries between parents and children are so permeable, stress reverberates across all boundary lines and family members live in a constant state of reactivity. One of the devastating results of enmeshment is when children get sucked emotionally into other's problems. If mom and dad are having marital problems, the kids know every sordid detail. Or, if dad isn't getting enough attention from mom, the children take on dad's despair. When a needy parent who is desperate for adult love turns to a child to supply it, that child becomes entangled in a web of dependency. Family therapists call this dynamic *loving down*, an appropriate word for children who are assigned to fill the emptiness of lonely adults.

In some enmeshed families, there is an emphasis on conformity and authority, sometimes with little concern for independence or privacy.[2] For example, if a daughter protests having her diary become an open book and says she needs her privacy, her mother might reply, "You're just a kid, what do you know about privacy?" Or, an adolescent who asks for an hour extension on his strict curfew hears from his father, "As long as you live in my house don't ever question my authority!"

As these children grow into adults, either they surrender their emotional and mental reality to whomever is in charge or they become so defiant that they are impossible to relate to. Either stance is a response to enmeshment and stems from reactivity and not from one's own integrity. Some adults

2. David Olson, *The Circumplex Model* (New York: Haworth Press, 1989).

raised in these families become enmeshed in their parents hopelessness and despair. It's not unusual for many adults to experience regular bouts of rage, depression or even paranoia because of this enmeshment. In other words, the path they are walking isn't their own and usually it takes some kind of crisis to find out who they really are and what choices they really want to make.

At the other extreme, disengaged families "do their own thing," with a characteristic lack of attachment or commitment among members of the family. In extremely disengaged families, the boundaries are so rigid that no response occurs, even when a response is necessary. Feelings of loyalty and closeness are lacking altogether. Problems within the family are denied because everyone acts as if nothing had ever happened. Sterile tradition takes the place of caring, and in the place of boundaries that enhance intimacy, walls are built between parent and child. In these families, individuals are so cut off from one another that warmth and caring cannot pass from one member to another. When crisis occurs, the mood vacillates between cool indifference to a sudden explosion of rage. If Johnny doesn't show up for dinner, no one seems to notice much or care. This family feels literally alone together and loneliness and isolation are an accepted way of life.

The film *Dead Poet's Society* is a perfect example of enmeshment. In the film, the son's feelings and aspirations are dictated by his father's wishes. The son's artistic talent is never valued nor is he allowed to savor achievement as his own. Eventually it leads to suicide, the ultimate way to break the crippling bind of enmeshment.

In contrast the disengaged family is exemplified by the passive, bloodless family portrait in *Ordinary People,* in which the mother's feelings have been paralyzed by the death of her oldest son, the darling of the family. Her emptiness forces her to keep everyone at a distance and to develop a family that keeps up appearances at all costs. It's excruciating to watch the family wall themselves off from their emotions, and see the results when their other son spends his life energy trying to keep his mother from her pain.

I'm not sure if any of us can quite comprehend the sacrifice involved when we are raised in families that are too enmeshed or disengaged. How can we create healthy boundaries when we lacked the warmth and vitality that flows from healthy family interactions? Many simply learn to sleepwalk through the pain, unconscious of their emotional, physical or spiritual needs. While unconscious, the family rules prevail. Obviously, the boundaries that are formed will be almost guaranteed not to serve our best interests. When we must surrender our reality to whomever is in charge, our beliefs and feelings are governed by what someone else wants us to believe or feel. As children we may be forced to adapt to such control, but as adults, such training causes us to walk a life path that is not our own. Some say that this forced march is the true definition of a crisis.

Creating a Sacred Reality

Healing boundaries begins when we decide to awaken and come back in touch with our own body and psyche, when finally we ask ourselves the right questions about the crippling styles we have adopted. Ultimately, we choose to be conscious of the rules that are the containers of our family patterns. What is so ironic, is that despite how we detested the rules at home, we tend to carry them unthinkingly into adulthood. These rules may be uncomfortable and even painful, but we continue to carry them with us like worn baggage. Like the little boy who runs away from home to escape his strict mother and just sits on the curb outside his house. When asked why he doesn't cross the street, the boy replies, "My mother told me not to!" When we think we can simply run away without doing our work, we find ourselves sitting on the curb, paralyzed by invisible loyalty. By the way, this has nothing to do with our intelligence. In fact, some of the brightest scholars are ignorant when it comes to their inherited family patterns.

I once was enrolled in an English class taught by a brilliant graduate student. He was a talented teacher but smiled constantly. His smile was pleasant, but sometimes it was incongruent with the subject matter and the rest of the expression on his face. It's hard to feel the impact of the death scene in *Romeo and Juliet* when it's being read by someone who's smiling. More bizarre were those times he was frustrated with the class and told us so with a raised voice . . . and a huge smile. His incongruent behavior reduced his credibility as an instructor. One day my friend received a failing grade on a final paper, with a note to see the teacher. I waited with her after class while she questioned the instructor about her grade. He responded with a grin, "This is the sloppiest paper I've ever read and I'm afraid you are failing this course." She was appalled by his incongruity and was assertive enough to ask how he could smile as he delivered this kind of an evaluation. She said that his expression felt like mockery. He was stunned and indicated that he didn't even know he was grinning!

Years later he and I became colleagues and we spoke about his experience as an instructor, and why he always smiled. He told me, sadly, that in his family pain wasn't tolerated. The rule was to keep that smile on your face! No matter what occurred, the children were expected to keep up appearances. He wasn't smiling any more that day when he told me that the muscles in his jaw had become so tight that he developed a medical problem!

Remember, *you can't leave the trap until you know you're in it* and releasing old rules demands that first you become aware of what you're carrying. Like anything else, it takes introspection and willingness to change. The following seven-step process can make you aware of the rules that govern your life, and help you discern how you want to exist in this world:

1. Make a list of life categories like money, sex, fun, decisions, men, women, friends, love, time, success, health, assertiveness, parenting, spirituality and whatever else you deem important.

2. Spend some time thinking of the rules that your family had about each category. Keep in mind that all families have rules, even if the rule was not to have any rules.

3. Go through each category and think about the rules you live by now. Are they the same as your family rules? Do your current rules work for you? Do you want to change or modify any, some, all of them?

4. Make a list of all the rules you want to keep, making any changes necessary.

5. On a separate page, list every rule that you want to release. These are the rules that serve no purpose or cause you pain. If you release old rules, you may need something to replace them. Think of some of the rules you received as a child, like, "children are to be seen and not heard", "don't cry or I'll give you something to cry about", or "do it like a lady!" Take each statement individually and change it into a statement that is loving, empowering and will serve your best interests.

   For example, "children are to be seen . . ." may become "I am entitled to give voice to my feelings." Instead of "don't cry . . ." try "my tears are healing and deserve expression." Instead of "do it like a lady" consider "I'll do it exactly the way I want."

6. Since old rules are deeply ingrained in our consciousness,

it's not particularly effective just to decide to throw them away. Instead, think of a ritual that will signify their release from your life. As silly as this sounds, ritual is important for us to ground our experience into sacred reality. Some people bury these toxic rules, others burn them or cast them into a lake or river. I worked with a woman who put her old rules in a helium balloon, invited her friends for a ceremony and released her old rules into the air.

Creating a comfort zone requires that we be intentional about choosing the rules we live by. We don't have to toss away every value from our families, but only create a reality for ourselves that is grounded in consciousness and not reaction. This is something we must do ourselves according to what beliefs we hold important, what kind of physical and emotional proximity is comfortable, and how we want to be in the world.

Some of what we choose will depend upon our spirituality, our religious beliefs and our thoughts about death. Certainly, if we cling to the idea of a heaven that admits only those who have adhered to rigid laws of conduct, then revising some of our laws will take a major restructuring of our beliefs. If we have the underlying conviction that suffering will be rewarded in the world to come, then no matter how many rules we make about embracing joy, we will cancel our order before it is placed!

It might take a spiritual emergency. A spiritual emergency is a term created by Christina Grof that describes a collision between how we've been living, and our longing for our true self and the sacred to emerge.[3] Sometimes it takes a literal Divine wake up call to inform us that the time has come for us to accept an invitation to grow again.

---

3. Christina Grof and Stanislav Grof, *Spiritual Emergency: When Personal Transformation Becomes a Crisis* (Los Angeles: Jeremy Tarcher, 1989).

8

The Decision to Heal

"The mystery can't be answered by repeating the question. Nor can it be bought by going to amazing places. Not until the eyes have been stilled and the desires quelled. Not until then can we cross over from confusion."

Rumi

I t is important to ask the right questions about our histories, primarily because it helps us to feel safer to know the origins of our pain. The patterns of the past are significant to the old images that we hold about ourselves. However, we need more to change our ways of being in the world because we know they no longer work for us.

We live in an analytical world where many people have become increasingly aware of their histories. However, knowing the past will not change our reactive patterns with others. Many of us in recovery can recite a litany of the past, but with very little insight into what needs to be done in the present to create a more expansive, fulfilling future. Some who have worked on themselves for years have become so vigilant about nearly every transaction they have that they wouldn't know their mental health if they tripped over it!

Our decision to heal our boundaries means that at some level we have decided to become conscious of our behavior and how we want to be treated. The resolve to become conscious is significant and courageous because it burns through the fog of denial and allows us to taste our pain as well as our joy. We experience the anguish of shame that is layered under justifications, rationalizations, dissociation and whatever other filters the brain can muster! From deep in our souls we heed a wake-up call that comes in forms not always pleasant, and we become willing to examine the boundaries, or lack thereof, that drove us to act contrary to our own values and integrity. This Divine intervention can come in the form of a painful relationship that can't be endured, an addiction that takes us to the bottom, a near death experience or a potentially lethal health problem. Sometimes it's the catastrophic ending of a relationship or a wounding that is so profound that we are literally forced to change the way we behave in order to survive. Occasionally I have witnessed those who have awakened because of a deep love that stirred their own inner knowing of who they are and how they want to be treated.

When these events occur, we are given an invitation to grow, to move beyond responding passively to life as if we are on automatic pilot. We become fully conscious of our feelings, thoughts and body cues and act congruently in ways that are life-giving not life-draining. At this juncture, we stop the rhetoric of recovery and enter into a new domain of freedom where our inner knowing is primary. In other words, we no longer decorate our jail cells, but we can actually leave the prison! The irony is that in some ways we have no choice. Mary Richards explains, "There is a spirit deep within all of us that is yearning to be free. And we may as well get out of its way, for it will give us no peace until we do." Many of us are all too aware that we will keep going through lessons again and again until we decide to change.

Healing our boundaries is not a casual endeavor that we undertake in our spare time. Those of us who decide to undertake this process know that the work demands our time, intention and dedication. Since we carry our boundaries with us to the workplace, to worship, in our intimate relationships and in our parenting, there is a synchronicity of healing that we must be aware of in all of our interactions. For example, I've known people who have done a great job of repairing their professional boundaries but maintain abusive behavior with friends and loved ones.

Judy works for a prestigious investment company and is quite skilled in what she does. However, she cannot control her anger when she becomes irritated at her office staff. The least mistake sets her off on a rampage. Judy has worked at this particular company for two years and has gone through four secretaries who were so put off by her abusive outbursts that they left. One day Judy came to work and was notified that unless she got some help with her rage, she was fired. Since her self-esteem was so wrapped up in her work, she decided to get some help learning how to contain her anger so she wouldn't lose her job.

Judy took classes in conflict resolution and meditation and used those new skills in her office. Her behavior improved and she was able to continue working. However, when she returned home at night she'd rage at her 14-year-old daughter for minor chores that weren't done correctly. Even though her emotional boundaries were intact at work, Judy felt entitled to continue her behavior with her loved ones, who put up with her behavior and maintained distant relationships with her. When her daughter ran away after one of her mother's outbursts, it was the wake-up call that Judy needed to discover the origins of her damaged boundaries and begin the healing process in all of her interactions.

When we can't contain our emotional and physical reactions,

there's an urgent need to create a comfort zone where we can regroup, breathe deeply and remember who we are. When we have no internal sacred space, it damages our soul. There are factors that may impede our decision to do the work that is necessary to create our well-being and safety. According to anthropologist Dr. Angeles Arrien, there are four cross-cultural "addictions" that lead to *soul-loss* and keep us immobilized in destructive patterns.[1] Of course as in any addiction, there is a gift that is waiting on the other side.

The four addictions are:

Addiction to intensity: *"If life is boring, I must not be truly living it. So I sensationalize, I dramatize and inflate myself and what is going on around me"*

This means that we add drama to our lives by living in the past and exaggerating our responses. Underneath, there is probably a strong need to be noticed and accepted. When we face our addiction to intensity, the gift that is waiting to be claimed is the gift of love and gratitude.

There is a story about a mother who was watching her three-year-old play in the park. Her son picked a flower to give to her and said, "Mom, you are so pretty, just like this flower!"

Mother took the flower and said, "That's nice. But why don't you ever tell me that you love me?"

When we confuse intimacy with intensity, we can't accept love when it comes to us. When we're fixated on how things are supposed to look, we can't create a comfort zone that will please us!

---

1. This material is included in A. Arrien's research which she has amplified and expanded into her educational training, *The Four-Fold Way: Walking the Paths of the Warrior, Teacher, Healer and Visionary,* (New York, HarperCollins, 1993.) For use of this material you must receive permission from the office of A. Arrien, P.O. Box 2077, Sausalito, CA 94966, 415-331-5050. All materials are copyrighted.

Addiction to perfection: *"I can't ever get this right, so I might as well give up!"*

Perfection doesn't tolerate mistakes. When we view the world through the lens of perfection, we lose our humanity and become so invested in roles that we begin to walk the procession of the living dead. When we are wrapped up in our need to be perfect, then any healing process will be undermined because we can never do it the right way! We expend tremendous amounts of energy in our search for perfection and any boundaries that we attempt to repair will be obliterated. What is waiting to be claimed on the other side is our own right use of energy, our personal power and our spirituality.

Addiction to our need to know: *"I have to learn everything about relationships before I ever have one."*

Beneath this compulsive need to figure it out is someone with a high need to control. If you grew up with chaos or abuse, it became necessary to try to reason why it was occurring. But this addiction can diminish our joy and keep us paralyzed. I've heard it said about adult children of alcoholics that if there was a door marked Heaven and a door marked Lecture About Heaven, most adult children would line up for the lecture. Needing to figure out our relationships, our work and our every transaction can become an excuse for nonaction. The information contained in any book is valuable only if it's put to use. What is waiting to be claimed is *our own inner wisdom and our own intuition and clarity.*

Addiction to our fixation of what's not working: *"I made so much progress on healing my boundaries and then something happens and I'm right back to the beginning again."*

When we are fixated on what's not working, we undermine our healing process with pessimism and then anything valuable we've achieved becomes a sham. This myopic view of the world will prevent us from appreciating what we've done when we encounter pitfalls in our progress, as we all will! We need to encompass the entire balance sheet of progress and setbacks, or we'll drown in discouragement. The gift that waits on the other side of this fixation is our own ability to bear fair witness to our lives and the lives of others, and our ability to look at the whole picture and achieve correct perspective.

Boundary work is about soul retrieval. Native cultures say that the remedies for soul retrieval are *singing, dancing, story telling, the creative arts and silence*. Discussion is of limited use in boundary work because boundaries are a mind-body phenomenon that calls for a physical response as well. Thus, we cannot forget to include these native remedies in any therapeutic process. Some of us experienced the beginning of soul loss in childhood when our boundaries and our sense of self became warped. Before you embark on your path of healing, I invite you to contemplate the following questions:

When in my life did I stop singing?
When in my life did I stop dancing?
When in my life did I stop being enchanted with my
    own story?
When in my life did I become uncomfortable with the
    sweet domain of silence?
When in my life did I stop creating?

Your answers will reveal when you started to experience soul loss. In my experience, this is also the time when any sense of self became diminished and we lost the ability to create any sanctuary that provided us with comfort.

The decision to create a comfort zone allows us to claim the disowned parts of ourselves that so desperately long to come home. The fear of abandonment, the anger of betrayal, the grief of profound loss will continue to haunt our relationships like souls that have died, but can't return to their Source. Dr. Raymond Charles Barker says, "Decision is the most important function of the individual mind. No creative process can begin until a decision is made."[2] I want to underscore that no one can make this decision for us. The time has come for us to take responsibility for ourselves and cease the suffering, the blaming and the violence that we do to ourselves and others. Our survival, and the survival of this planet rests on this decision.

---

2. Raymond Charles Barker, *The Power of Decision,* (New York: Perigee Books, 1991).

Boundaries for All Occasions: Creativity in Action

"The greatest discovery of any generation is that human beings can alter their lives by altering their attitudes of mind."

Albert Schweitzer

O ne afternoon I was getting ready to go to a meeting that I dreaded. I knew I'd see a particular woman with whom I was negotiating who was pushy and intimidating. She insisted continually that her ideas were correct and had an obnoxious way of doing so. I acquiesced to her demands out of sheer exhaustion! On this particular day I had been writing about intellectual and emotional boundaries and I decided that it would be refreshing to practice what I was preaching. As I finished putting on my suit, it occurred to me that—physically preparing for the meeting—I needed to complete my mental preparation as well. To be fully prepared for this occasion, I needed the appropriate boundaries.

As I drove to the meeting, I decided what I needed first was to maintain an emotional boundary. Wearing vulnerability and fear just didn't fit for this meeting and certainly didn't add to my comfort. I determined that a stronger boundary was needed, so I chose my firm emotional boundary highlighted with subtle tones of flexibility. This felt more appropriate, and certainly went well with my dark blue business suit. Since I wanted to hear her opinions but not surrender to them, my intellectual screening device would be a sturdy, fine mesh that I could use for discernment. This mesh could be cleaned easily so I could let in the ideas that fit and discard the ideas that did not. My outfit was complete with a clear Plexiglas physical boundary that I could employ in case she started pushing her face into mine to make her point.

Finally, instead of picturing this woman looming over me in vivid color with a booming voice, I choose to imagine her as a small black and white image with a voice like Minnie Mouse. It wasn't so difficult at this point to picture myself in clear, vivid, life-size color speaking to a small, dull woman with a squeaky voice. I started to relax and even felt amused as I drove into the parking lot, parked and gathered my things.

When I walked into the meeting I felt more comfortable and prepared than I had the previous day. I was able to tell her politely to back off when she was in my physical space. As the discussion heated up and I felt my fear coming to the foreground, I took a break and used the time to soothe myself and step into my emotional comfort zone again. When the meeting was finally over, we were both satisfied with the compromises. As she was leaving, she turned to me and said, "You know, I thought you would be a push over, most people are quite intimidated by me. But I like your style! Let's get together and have lunch!"

I left the meeting with the unmistakable knowing that I didn't want to spend another minute with her, but also I left with a sense of empowerment. When I am intentional about my boundaries, I can create an internal environment that serves my best interests.

There are internal boundaries for every situation we encounter. We can decide the intensity and vulnerability we take in, or show to others. The challenge is to know what resources we've got and how to use them. We've been provided with a veritable buffet of options. As in my story, there are different hues and textures available to us. Depending on the situation, our memory of similar situations, our gender and our cultural background, we will employ different combinations of boundary patterns to suit our needs.

Learning to make decisions in our own best interest is something that many of us didn't learn as children. If so, it's imperative that we begin now to use our creativity in ways that serve us well. All of us had creative energy as children. Now that we are grown, we may believe that this ability is either gone, or this energy is reserved only for certain areas of our life. Not true! Creativity doesn't disappear, but it can atrophy from disuse.

To use our creative capabilities we need to be willing to learn how to change our experiences in useful ways. If your boundaries, or lack of boundaries, aren't working for you, it might be time to try something else. Most of us have a perverse tendency to continue doing something out of habit, even if it doesn't work. Not only that, but we continue to use the same strategy, only we try harder, longer and more often. It reminds me of a parent's response to a child who doesn't understand something. It is not uncommon to see frustrated parents mindlessly shout the same sentence over again instead of trying a new set of words.

It's ironic that we will spend time and money to improve our physical appearance, but internally we are disheveled and anxious. When we approach any situation feeling intimidated, anxious and obsessed with failure, our boundaries automatically become too permeable or unbelievably rigid. In the previous story, if I had not prepared myself internally for my morning meeting, I would have short circuited the entire encounter before it even began! It's amazing when we realize that it takes the same amount of time to drive ourselves crazy as it does to do some advance planning and re-create our experiences in positive ways.[1]

Years ago I worked with a couple who were very much in love but always seemed to come together at the end of the day and fight. Both of them had extremely stressful jobs and often left work feeling harried and overwhelmed. They had become so used to conflict in their home that each of them came prepared for a fight the minute they walked in the door. Of course, they each knew just how to trigger each other's hurt and anxiety and would unconsciously do so within moments of their initial greeting. Their boundary styles were very different and often exacerbated the conflict. Her tendency was to run away and his tendency was to charge ahead. A perfect match!

I asked the woman how she felt when she was driving home at the end of the day. She said her shoulders would tighten and her gut would start to ache as she came closer to her home. By the time she turned into the driveway she was filled with dread and ready to run in her bedroom and lock the door. When I asked her how she pictured her husband as she drove home, she said that she imagined him pacing the floor with an angry expression on his face about something "she didn't do right."

Her husband had much the same physical response on the way home, but pictured his wife being withdrawn and withholding any warmth. This image provoked such hurt in him that often he was surly when he walked in. It was clear that

---

1. Richard Bandler, *Using Your Brain for a Change* (Moab, Utah: Real People Press, 1985).

both of them spent so much time agonizing about their initial greeting that there was absolutely no way either of them could get their needs met.

In order to begin to arrest this reoccurring scene, this couple had to learn to prepare themselves for a different kind of encounter while driving home. Both of them began to practice relaxing their gut, dropping their shoulders, unclenching their teeth and breathing deeply. (When we are scrunched up in a ball of tension, it is difficult to see the world as a friendly place.) This meant that instead of listening to the news or using their car phones, they would choose to put on some soothing music or drive in silence. While driving home, I asked the woman to picture her husband wearing his work clothes and sitting on the floor blowing bubbles with peanut butter all over his face. I also invited her to choose the boundaries that she would like to wear for her entrance into the house. Instead of her usual suit of armor, she began to imagine a textured screen that had openings that could be made wider or smaller depending on the circumstances. Since she loved the smell of fresh flowers, she decided that inside her screen was a small garden filled with the scent of roses.

The husband and I worked on a different image and he became intentional about changing his expectations about the encounter before he arrived home. He learned that too often expectations are resentments waiting to happen, and he could stop sabotaging himself by being more open to outcome rather than fixated on a particular response. It was important for him to contain his anger and be vulnerable about any hurt he was experiencing. It was also a *strong* option for both of them to take some time separately after work so that they could relax and step into their comfort zone.

Obviously, changing ingrained patterns of boundaries and behaviors takes time and patience. But until we attend to the images we carry and the stories we create in our minds, we will continue to be undisciplined about our responses. For those who wish to prepare themselves for situations in which boundaries tend to be too permeable or rigid, the following is a list of Neuro-Linguistic Programming techniques. These are visual, kinesthetic and auditory elements that can be used to assist in creating a state of relaxation and empowerment.[2]

Color: Picture the impending scene and vary the intensity from bright colors to black and white.

Distance: Change the image in your mind from very close to far away.

Depth: Vary the picture of yourself or the participants from a flat, two dimensional photo to the full depth of three dimensions.

Clarity: Picture what your boundaries may look like. Then, change the picture from crystal-clear clarity to fuzzy indistinctness. For those who wish to strengthen their boundaries, imagine just the opposite.

Speed: Adjust the speed of the scene from very fast to very slow.

Transparency: Make any image in the scene transparent, so that you can see what's beneath the surface.

For you who are not visual and have difficulty picturing a scene, here are some different elements that you can utilize in your imagination:

Auditory: Change the pitch, volume, tonality or duration of the sounds or voices in the situation in order

---

2. Bandler, 24.

to de-escalate conflict. Or strengthen your own voice or alter the sounds of other voices.

Kinesthetic: Vary the temperature of the environment, the movement of the scene or even the texture of your boundaries, from cold steel to soft clouds, or vice versa. Imagine how you want your physical and emotional boundary to feel.

Olfactory: Experiment with pleasing and/or powerful odors and tastes you want to permeate this scene. For example, in a given situation where you usually leave with a "bad taste in your mouth," make sure that the taste will be pleasing to you. Odors and tastes are very powerful anchors for the imagination!

To experiment with these elements, think of a past experience that was pleasant. Remember to breathe and notice the areas of tension in your body. As you imagine this pleasant memory, change the brightness of the image and notice how your feelings change in response. When you have done this, begin to make the image dimmer until you can barely see it. There are always exceptions to any example, but for most people, making the image brighter usually intensifies the feelings, while decreasing the brightness decreases the intensity.

Now, try experimenting with the size of the image. Sometimes, when we blow things out of proportion, it is a literal description of what we're feeling. Again, there are exceptions, but if you change the size of an unpleasant picture, you will most likely find that making it smaller also decreases your reactions. For some of us, making an image quite large either makes it laughable or more frightening. The idea here is to find out what works for you by trying *one* element at a time and noticing your response. *There is no right or wrong way to do this,* and since safety is primary, don't do anything that feels too frightening or dangerous.

It is possible to change our perceptions of an experience by preparing our state of mind.[3] Rather than being a quick fix, this is a way to soothe ourselves so that we can enter situations with more comfort and protection. It's up to us to change the patterns that undermine our dignity. When we can take responsibility for our healing, the results will be empowering.

---

3. Richard Bandler and John Grinder, *Reframing: Neuro-Linguistic Programming and the Transformation of Meaning* (Moab, Utah: Real People Press, 1982).

10

Mending
Body
and Soul

"I step into the day
I step into myself
I step into the mystery"

Ojibwa Prayer

T hus far I have discussed many of the factors that make it difficult to set boundaries. Many of these stem from our childhood and have their origins in the kind of attachments we had and the ways we were treated. The fear of disapproval, the fear of abandonment or the sense that we are not entitled to our limits are a few common reasons that keep us immobilized. For survivors of abuse, it may be the feeling that our bodies don't belong to us and our inability to discern that our boundaries actually are being violated until after the intrusion is over. For some of us it's shame or guilt that prevent us from setting limits because we feel so defective that literally we can't take a stand in support of our dignity. Whatever the origin in each case, we still pay the price when we fail to take care of ourselves and set limits.

We can begin by discerning what situations and people

threaten our boundaries and what we do that is based on childhood distortions of the present. However, until we can look at the shame we carry, rarely will we experience the blessing of healthy interactions in our lives. Shame can get in the way of our being accountable and taking action. Shame is a primary symptom, an indication that our boundaries have been violated in some way. When we internalize shame, either we become shameful or shameless. Thus, I could be shameless about my intrusive behavior and feel entitled to act however I want. Or, if I'm shameful about my intrusive boundaries, I may feel deficient, bad and generally paralyzed to do anything about it. Chances are, people won't confront me about my boundaries because of my shame, so I blame myself or shame someone else and that's where it stops. For those who are immobilized by shame so it contaminates their healing process, the following ideas may help.

1. When shame occurs, learn to recognize it by noticing how your body feels: sinking feeling in your chest, nausea, warm face, etc.
2. Identify the behaviors you resort to when you protect yourself from your shame: eating, smoking, drinking, attacking, anger, silence, etc.
3. Learn to identify what you're feeling: Oh, my chest is tight I must be shaming myself again.
4. Take a moment and reflect on the interactions of the day. Has someone violated your boundaries, or have you violated someone else's boundaries?
5. Learn to counteract a shame attack by turning from internal to external: count the change in your pocket, count the cars going down the street, put on your Walkman and listen to some music, use meditation to relax.

6. Practice neutralizing shame by giving yourself soothing affirmations.
7. Re-connect with safe people as soon as possible.

When you discover the origins of your boundary damage, you are able to have compassion for yourself and don't feel so crazy when you slip into old behavior. So, no matter what stage of growth you're in, please appreciate how far you have come. Healing is a cyclical process and sometimes we return to the same themes only to be healed at a deeper, more sophisticated level. Please, be gentle and patient with yourself.

It's crucial to look at your boundary formation as fluid and changeable depending upon the situation, the interaction and your intention. It is helpful to picture an energy field around you that is vibrant and healthy and can be deployed at any time from within you. Take a few minutes before you start each day to envision the following image:

Picture an orb of light that exists within your solarplexus. The energy is friendly, pulsating and ready to be used for your protection when you need it. Feel this wonderful energy that is vital, warm and has been with you since you were born into this world.

Say to yourself:

This life energy radiates from me. It is filled with love
and strength and contains within in it all that I need to
protect myself from harm. I can modulate this energy
out of my perfect knowing of who I am and what I need.
When I am in danger, I send out this brilliant energy that
surrounds me and allows me to keep myself safe. When
I want to be close to someone, I can change the intensity
of this energy and include someone in this force field
and surround us both with warm comfortable light.

No one exists within my energy who is not safe. As I
scan the people and situations that exist in my life, I
now release those who consciously or unconsciously
seek to do me harm. I surround my self with this loving
vital energy that allows me to see with perfect clarity
those situations that are worthy of my attention and
participation and those situations that are now complete and need to be released. I trust my body, my
mind and my spirit to guide me.

In repairing our boundaries, we need to know some of the
loyalties we carry with us that may be intergenerational. Out
of loyalty to family members, we may unconsciously allow
ourselves to be violated. For those who have done a great deal
of personal growth, the ideas presented in this book may be
something you've struggled with for a very long time. If this
is the case, and you are still grappling with the same old
boundary issues, you might consider that you are still being
loyal to parents or to a family system who at some level does
not want you to change. Remember, anxious attachments are
the most addictive patterns to undo, and even though you
may know a lot of data, people rarely make decisions based on
information. If they did, there would be no smokers, no
drunk drivers and a whole host of self destructive behaviors
would be eliminated!

When we start to change our behavior, particularly with
family members, we may feel disloyal as if we were betraying
someone by becoming healthy. If we do something good for
ourselves but feel shameful about it, we must ask ourselves to
whom we are still being loyal? If we feel loyal to a perpetrator, then we must get the support we need to give voice to our
wounds. If we experience perpetual confusion and indecision
about what to do about our boundaries, perhaps we need to
ask ourselves who taught us that we can't see clearly and

make decisions in our own best interest? When we discover
our loyalty issues, we are able to unpack the intergenerational
shame that has kept us stuck in a cycle of suffering. It is also
possible that as we uncover these patterns of loyalty we may
experience anger or intense sadness as we set about strength-
ening our identity.

Ivan Boszormenyi-Nagy, author of *Invisible Loyalties*, suggests that we are born into this world with family debts and
credits that go back generations. Out of unconscious loyalty,
we sometimes find ourselves paying back old family debts and
are often miserable while we are doing it.[1] A useful exercise
for those who can't set limits is to make a list of the positive
aspects that you were born with and the possible debts that
you are paying back for family members that you may not be
aware of. It's very possible that as you begin to heal your
boundaries, you may run up against powerful family debts
that make it virtually impossible to change until they become
overt and available to your consciousness.

Marie and Susan became friends a year ago. Susan is
Jewish and Marie grew up in a small German Catholic town
and was fascinated with Susan's heritage. These two women
shared a love of cooking and decided to open a catering business. Marie was relatively happy in her new career except
that she was unable to set appropriate limits with her business
partner. Susan would ask Marie for money and then not pay
her back, she would borrow Marie's car to run a business
errand that would normally take an hour and then return the
car several hours later with the gas tank on empty. It wasn't
uncommon to see Susan smoking in the office when Marie
had repeatedly asked her not to.

---

1. Ivan Boszormenyi-Nagy and Geraldine M. Spark, *Invisible Loyalties* (New York:
   Harper & Row, 1973).

Marie is assertive and confident in her dealings with her friends and her clients and could not understand why she let Susan walk all over her. Every time she set out to confront Susan, she felt guilty and suppressed her anger or acquiesced to Susan's behavior. Marie became resentful and dreaded going to work so much that she contemplated leaving the business. Several weeks later she was visiting her mother and shared her dilemma concerning Susan. Marie's mother asked if that was her daughter's "Jewish friend." Her mother made the strange statement that "this family has a history with Jews." Marie listened as her mother told her the story of what happened in Germany during World War II.

Apparently, Marie's grandmother was hiding a Jewish woman from the Nazis and was forced to turn her out into the streets of Munich because it became too dangerous to keep her. This woman was raped and killed and Marie's grandmother never forgave herself. Unconsciously, Marie was repaying a debt for her family by allowing Susan to take advantage of her. With this knowledge, Marie felt the sadness and shame that was wrapped in such secretiveness for so many years. With her understanding, she was gradually able to begin the task of setting limits with Susan so that she could continue working with her.

Most of us know too well that to decide to change is to step into the uncertainty of chaos for a time. An anonymous 15th century Hasidic rabbi eloquently describes this chaos when he writes:

> "Nothing in the world can change from one reality to another until it turns into nothing. And then it is made into a new creature, from the egg to the chick. The moment when the egg is no more and the chick is not yet, is nothingness. The primal state which precedes creation is called chaos."

We need to understand that changing behavior naturally engenders confusion. Changing our agreements and limits with others means that we will enter into a period of awkwardness and disorientation commonly known as transition. We must be patient with our process and quiet the critical voices that impede our growth. Wherever we are, whatever our state of adjustment and growth, we didn't get here overnight, and we won't correct our course overnight. A therapist friend says that any time a client asks, "How long will this take?" she always answers, "How long were you a child?"

Paul Watzlawick tells us that we are at our most disoriented state just before we make a major change in our lives.[2] Any time we let go of an old situation, relationship, identity or behavior, we suffer the confusion of in-betweeness. When we choose to change our boundaries we are faced with an end of old behavior followed by a period of confusion or distress that leads to new beginnings. We must honor each part of this journey. Be aware that the process of disorientation to re-orientation marks the turning points on our paths to growth. In a patriarchal society, transition is not honored. We know about goals and goal setting, but what happens in between is ignored and so we aren't taught the importance of this process.

It is during transition when the most significant changes occur. It is a test of faith to believe that we will indeed grasp the future and be able to pull ourselves to safety. Martin Buber called God "the space in-between."[3] This period of transition is a very sacred space where our faith and our courage can be revealed.

---

2. Paul Watzlawick, et al, *Change: Principles of Problem Formation and Problem Resolution* (New York: Norton, 1974).

3. Martin Buber, *I and Thou* (New York: Scribner, 1978).

Healing our physical, emotional, intellectual and spiritual boundaries demands both internal and external work. The internal process has to do with introspection and can be initiated by examining our desires, our likes and dislikes, especially those that don't depend on the messages you received from family, friends and intimate others. It's helpful to keep a journal and take time to contemplate what was pleasing or displeasing about your day. When you discover your desires, you can begin to make decisions that are based on your knowing rather than what's deemed important by others.

It's imperative to breath deeply and notice when you block your own impulses through body posture or holding your breath. This is the key factor in developing healthy boundaries. The way I know I'm being invaded is registered in my gut, my temperature and my muscle tension. I will be unaware of all these cues if I don't breathe. In order to listen to our nonverbal signals, we need to develop an attitude of respect for our bodies.

Physical boundaries. We may begin by considering the following questions. There are no right or wrong answers.

Do you generally like to be touched?
Who are the people from whom you want touch?
If someone knows you well, where can they touch you?
What kinds of touch feel affectionate to you?
What kinds of touch feel sexual?
What kinds of touch are repulsive to you?
How do you let people know if they come too close to
    you?
Where in your body do you feel a reaction when some-
    one comes too close?
How do you signal to people to come closer?
Where in your body do you feel it?
When you want affection from someone and they

continue to distance, what are your options?
What are the nonverbal cues that others give that signal that they're not safe? e.g., tight jaw, clenched
fist, stance, stare?

Emotional boundaries can be discerned through our
responses to others. When emotional boundaries are damaged,
we become reactive, we see emotions as indulgences or we try
to numb our emotions by addictions or other self-destructive
behaviors. The following are suggestions to consider for healing emotional boundaries.

1. If someone demands information about how you feel, be
   true to your self and respond only if it feels appropriate.
   If you aren't sure, take the time you need.
2. Raging and condemnation are forms of emotional abuse.
   If this happens, you don't have to stay and be a container for someone else's emotional "garbage."
3. If you tend to rage, learn to notice your feelings of hurt
   or shame that precede your outbursts. Take time to
   soothe yourself through meditation, relaxation, exercise, music, affirmations, etc.
4. It's important to find another adult who is safe to talk
   with when you are hurting, angry or resentful.
5. If you're in an intimate relationship, you can learn to
   contain your anger and express it appropriately by saying: I want . . .
   I resent . . .
   I appreciate . . .
6. If certain emotions are consistently overwhelming, it
   may be productive to investigate if you were enmeshed
   in your parents' emotions that were irresponsibly
   expressed or denied.

Intellectual boundaries are limits or rules that are learned. To change the pattern of our perceptions, we need to learn to value our inner wisdom and intuition. The following suggestions may help to strengthen our intellectual boundaries.

1. You are the expert on your thoughts. If someone insists that they can read your mind, it is time to exit quickly.
2. If you don't trust your perceptions, ask those you trust to validate or give feedback on your experience.
3. You can be discerning about whether what you are told is true. It is important to weigh information before you make it your own.
4. It's probable that others have insights that you don't have.
5. If you're too busy managing your feelings to take in any information, it's important to take time to calm down.

Spiritual Boundaries. Creating boundaries for ourselves is part of our spiritual work. Most of us must create a safe container before we can bring the blessings of spirituality into our lives. When we can empower ourselves by intentionally choosing our boundaries, we experience dignity, self-respect and we are able to give and receive love in ways that nurture our souls and enhance our serenity.

Your responses to the following questions will get you started on your path to healthy spirituality.

1. What behavior do I use that undermines my sense of self?
2. What are the behaviors that I use with others that diminish my dignity and self-respect?
3. How do I sustain my serenity when others attempt to shame me in overt or covert ways?

4. What brings me in touch with the in-dwelling Divine?[4]

Wanting to know who we are beyond the rules and regulations that have kept us safe is essential for repairing emotional boundaries. To establish healthy boundaries, it's
important to slow down and learn the language of our body
cues. As many of us grew from childhood into adulthood, we
began to ignore our bodies and learned to focus our attention
on the intellectual domain. We need to trust our body signals
just as we depend on our thoughts and our perceptions.
When we are blocked from experiencing either, this is when
our lives become out of balance.

When learning any new skill, we need to practice it until
we know it with our body, mind and soul. This means that we
must open the doors to alternative possibilities of healing like
breath work, body work, movement, art and other expressive
therapies. Just as there are many ways to be wounded, there
also are many ways to achieve healing. Sometimes, it just isn't
productive to sit in therapy and discuss our trauma. When our
bodies have been violated, we need other methods.

"Every movement is preceded by support," says Bonnie
Bainbridge-Cohen.[5] To move, our hands use muscle, bone,
connective tissue and brain impulses. If we have a muscle
injury that restricts movement, a physical therapist would
begin work on the support mechanisms that enable hand
movement. If that therapist went right for the painful muscle,
the muscle would spasm and add to the pain and constricted
mobility. We can use this metaphor to assist us in the healing

4. To refresh your memory about spiritual boundaries, return to Chapter 2, "Creating a
   Safe Container," pages 16-17, and "Boundary Violations," pages 76-79.
5. Bonnie Bainbridge-Cohen, *Sensing, Feeling and Action: Experiential Anatomy of
   Body-Mind Centering* (Body-Mind Centering Institute, 1981).

of our boundaries. This notion, however, is contrary to what is sanctioned in Western culture. That when something is wrong we go right to the source and "fix it."

For example, if I were working with a sexual abuse survivor who had never talked about her issues with another human being, I wouldn't send her to a massage therapist as a first step of treatment. Undoubtedly she has learned to dissociate and needs to come back into her body to discover her limits. However, touch probably would produce such anxiety for her that it could reactivate the trauma if begun too soon. Prescribing or initiating body contact as the first step in healing her boundaries would be unethical and irresponsible. The effect would be similar to massaging a sore muscle.

The place to start is to determine if you are a boundary distancer or a boundary intruder. Do you tend to have permeable boundaries that are inclined to be violated, or are your boundaries so rigid that you can't let others in emotionally, physically or intellectually? Or a combination of both? Perhaps your emotional boundaries are rigid, but you have physical boundaries that are too diffuse. Perhaps your perceptual boundaries are so guarded that you become oblivious and defensive to others' ideas or feedback, but you become like an emotional sponge to others' emotions. It is imperative to realize that what may be acceptable boundary patterns to one person, may be completely unacceptable to another. When doing boundary work, it's not uncommon to find one women who goes to the dentist and feels sexually violated when the dentist drills her teeth, while another regularly participates in sexual fantasies with her Clergyman and doesn't consider that a boundary violation!

Remember, the issue here is safety. We need to feel safe to change our boundary patterns and, consequently, our behavior. Our patterns were developed because of our need to protect ourselves against abandonment, rejection, abuse and a whole host of interactions with an environment that wasn't always safe for us as children. Therefore, it makes no sense to unwrap the containers that have kept us functioning until we can create the kind of secure atmosphere that promotes growth. It's particularly disconcerting to see men and women with diffuse boundaries enter into behaviors that are not in their best interest because they have surrendered their reality to a healer, shaman, breath-worker, clergy or therapist who is in charge. We are the expert on our boundaries. Even though new behavior sometimes is necessary, we need to take care of ourselves by checking out suggestions that don't feel right.

In the final analysis we have limited control in the ways we can manipulate our environment. Where we can exert some control is how we tune into our inner world and create a safe harbor. Adults who have boundary problems need to be able to soothe themselves to feel a sense of safety. We who are attempting this courageous effort may want to use some form of meditation to create a safe inner sanctuary as a beginning to this healing work.

Here are guidelines for setting limits:

1. There are no perfect limits.
2. Our task is to be aware of who we are and how we feel in a given situation.
3. We are responsible for being clear about what we will or won't tolerate.
4. We have the right to set limits for ourselves so that we can feel safe.
5. We can have fun, maintain intimacy and still set limits that are right for us.
6. We don't have to stay in unhealthy relationships or situations.
7. We don't have to take it personally or think there's

something wrong with us when someone else is setting
their limits.

As we change our patterns, there can be times when we
feel overwhelmed with grief and sadness. Saying goodbye to
some of the old dynamics that provided us with the illusion
of safety may be a catalyst to feelings of betrayal and loss.
Allowing ourselves to grieve will help us to let go. I hope that
all who endeavor this healing process will welcome their
tears and know that these tears can be the antiseptic to their
wounds. Rather than using the Judeo-Christian ethic of a
clean heart, I prefer the Native American perspective of
keeping a moist heart. Native wisdom holds that the soil of
the human heart is watered by tears, that our tears keep the
ground soft and from this ground new life grows.

We are not alone on this healing journey. We can find help
and support, discover the value of sharing our journey with
others who are also struggling to create their comfort zone.
Then we can rejoice with those who rejoice, and mourn with
those who mourn. The experience of that kind of community
is life-saving and life-giving.

CHAPTER

11

Hold That Feeling and I'll Express It for You: Projective Identification and Bonding Patterns

> *"We meet ourselves time and again in a thousand disguises on the paths of life."*
>
> Carl Jung

hen couples claim that they share everything, often they're declaring more than they realize. Those who have participated in group therapy probably have witnessed the phenomenon called *projective identification* (PI). One afternoon a colleague came to consult with me about his sexual abuse survivor's group. In the previous session a young man came to group to tell his story about being victimized by his father. He told his story in a controlled, unemotional manner. Within minutes, the entire group became enraged and grief stricken. Meanwhile, the fellow who brought the story to the group displayed very little emotion. After the group was over, the man commented to the therapist that perhaps this group was not for him.

"Why?" asked my colleague.

"They're all so emotional. I think they have a lot of work to do on themselves!"

When we disown, repress or dissociate from our feelings, our partners, group members or even employees who have weak emotional boundaries will assume the responsibility of expressing them for us. The man who wanted to leave the group above is unaware that his disowned emotions were being taken on by the group members. If he has a love relationship, probably the same covert arrangement works there, too.

Intimate relationships are particularly vulnerable to projective identification. If you're in a relationship where you start interactions feeling calm and comfortable and inevitably feel afraid, anxious or angry, this dynamic may be at work. Or, have you ever looked back in your relationship and observed that you used to be so very anxious and afraid most of the time, but as you got closer, your partner became so anxious and jittery that now it drives you nuts? Not only that, but you wonder why you hadn't noticed it before. This pattern is so insidious that even trained clinicians who work with this all the time become prey to PI if they aren't cautious.

I remember working with a woman with a dissociative disorder. She could recall earlier events but was completely disconnected from her feelings. After one session with her it became clear that I had to step into my emotional boundary before the session or I'd be carrying her grief the rest of the day! Sometimes I've thought that if this transfer of emotions were a conscious process, we could make arrangements beforehand to express someone else's feelings and charge a small fee. Wouldn't it be interesting to see a prenuptial agreement saying:

"I, Judy, will hold the anger in this relationship and my beloved, George, promises to express it for me at the rate of $10.00/hour plus gratuities."

If this were the case, the husband in the following story would become a very wealthy man!

Judy grew up in a household in northern Michigan where expressions of emotion were unwelcome and repressed. Her parents kept their emotions under a close rein and expected the same from their children. Consequently, family life was always as cold as the frigid winters.

Judy was shamed if she expressed anger and warned if she appeared too joyful. She grew into a quiet young adult whose outward calm hid a storm of unexpressed feeling. The rigid discipline in her family produced great determination in her. Some would have called her stubborn, but it helped her get what she wanted.

Ultimately, she wanted George, a sometime writer who never seemed to know what he wanted and who looked to Judy to give his life practical direction. A few short months after they married, people noticed that George had become a more aggressive person. Judy seemed to provoke him to stage tantrums in public places and then shrug her shoulders at this behavior, as it to say, "It is not my fault. I didn't know he was like this!" Although once he'd been afraid to voice any critical opinion, soon George became critical of everyone, while Judy watched his displays of temper serenely, even with the appearance of relief. Unconsciously, she had shifted her disowned anger onto her partner who now could express her forbidden feelings and take the blame. Her unconscious choice had now become his problem.

This dynamic is more common than we might imagine. In fact it's quite clear that we are attracted to people who can collude with us in this way. I love the word collusion because it means literally co-illusion. It takes two people to partici-pate in the co-illusion of projective identification. Some-times it seems even that two people are made for each other because of this dynamic. It's helpful to understand that both members of the relationship have damaged boundaries, other-wise this dynamic couldn't be activated.

Although it may be convenient to have your significant other express your uncomfortable or forbidden feelings, in the long run it doesn't serve you well. Studies in bio-psycho-immunology, the mind/body connection, demonstrate the somatic results of repressed feelings: if we don't scream, our bodies will! That fact, combined with the enormous toll that PI takes on our relationships, are reasons enough to repair the holes in our emotional comfort zone. Healing begins with the resolve to be honest in all interactions. With honesty we not only begin to transcend our childhoods problems, we also stop putting our unfinished business onto our partners.

When we disown certain parts of ourselves that we don't like or can't tolerate, those parts have control over us. In practicing the art of relationship, we need to welcome all our parts into our comfort zone. This doesn't mean that we have to display our rage or anxiety in every interaction. Rather, we need to acknowledge its presence and learn to use the energy productively. If we don't own them, they will intrude into how we connect with others.

News Flash!
Anxious Girl Meets Angry Father!

Our bonding patterns develop early in reaction to our emotional environment. Beginning in childhood we developed strategies to defend our vulnerability.[1] Our defense strategy was imperative for our survival, particularly if our parents couldn't tolerate our emotions or didn't like who we

---

1. Hal Stone and Sidra Winkelman, *The Dance of the Selves in Relationship*, (Audiotape, 1990).

were. Since none of us had perfect parents, most of us have cultivated a primary persona that is our most developed part and that aspect we show most often to the world. When we begin to trust and feel safe with another person, we may consciously or unconsciously allow different parts of our personality to emerge. I will refer to these aspects of personality as *ego states* or *subpersonalities*. These are the vulnerable parts of ourselves, the parts we feel need to be hidden to make us acceptable to others and to feel safe in the world.

Most of us have had the experience of being "taken over" by a part of ourselves that we didn't know was there.[2] We are a crowd inside. There may be a needy inner child, a critical parent, a raging bully and even a seductress. These aspects of ourselves come into play at various times and for various reasons. In fact, Dr. James Fadiman suggests that one possible definition for mental illness is the wrong personality, at the wrong time, doing the wrong thing.[3]

For those who have experienced hideous abuse or have witnessed violence as children, these ego states become encapsulated and are unavailable to consciousness except through concentrated inner work. However, most of us are aware of the different ego states or parts of ourselves that make up the complex orchestra of our personality. The question is, who is the conductor?

Max, a successful bank officer, has a primary persona that reflects confidence, control and lack of emotion. However, when he feels hurt and criticized, there is a part of him that behaves like an angry fourteen year old. When this happens, Max lashes out at those who are closest to him. There is also

---

2. John Rowan, *Subpersonalities: The People Inside Us* (New York: Routledge, 1990).
3. James Fadiman, "The Many Parts of the Self." (International Conference of Transpersonal Psychology, Prague Czechoslovakia, 1991).

a terrified ego state in him that remembers his father's bankruptcy. At the age of four, Max lived in scarcity, not sure from day to day if he would have a roof over his head. This is the part of Max that doesn't tolerate uncertainty. If plans aren't finalized or if people don't do what they say they will do, Max becomes curt, abrupt and so anxious that he looks as if he will explode. Neither of these ego states show themselves unless Max feels hurt, vulnerable, anxious or scared. In fact, these ego states were so contrary to the way Max saw himself and so abhorrent to him that he was basically unconscious of his reactions. This worked well for him until he began a relationship with Yvonne.

Yvonne's primary persona was charming, gregarious and flighty. She appeared to be optimistic and carefree. In reality, when she became vulnerable she felt scared and anxious. Any signal of abandonment could send her into a tailspin of anxiety and depression.

After two months of dating, Max and Yvonne were puzzled how a relationship that started so beautifully could turn so miserable. Max thought that Yvonne was the essence of warmth and caring. He was disarmed by her effusive, charming manner and her spontaneity which he found refreshing and delightful, until that spontaneity became the bane of his existence!

Yvonne, on the other hand admired Max's cool demeanor and confidence. She felt comforted by his quiet strength and gladly allowed Max to be in charge. Until that cool demeanor turned withholding and oppressively controlling. She wondered what happened to the quiet, confident man who turned out to have regular bouts of rage and sullenness.

Whenever Yvonne changed her mind about plans that involved Max, he'd get angry. Gradually he became wounded by Yvonne's spontaneity and saw it as thoughtless and inconsiderate. After any incident, he'd spend the next two days sulking, and convincing himself that if Yvonne really loved him she wouldn't do this "changing around bit." Also, it wasn't uncommon for Max to threaten to leave her when he felt hurt. Of course, Yvonne took the threat to heart and became hysterical. During these times she acted like a needy child, begging for his approval. Ironically, Yvonne got so anxious when she thought Max was leaving her that she forgot details about plans they had made together or agreements that she had made earlier. Naturally, this reinforced Max's hurt and consequently Yvonne's anxiety. Their constant struggling choked all joy out of their relationship. They loved each other dearly, but loving wasn't enough to salvage their relationship.

Max and Yvonne were locked into bonding patterns that controlled their interactions and caused a chain reaction they couldn't seem to control. Max's "critical, angry father" got locked into Yvonne's "anxious little girl." So when Max felt hurt, he became angry and critical and in response Yvonne got anxious and felt like a child. Max feared he wasn't loved, Yvonne feared Max would leave. Since nothing could be resolved when this couple was locked into this pattern, their hurt, anger and anxiety only escalated. The scene replayed like a broken record and had contaminated their relationship to such an extent that interactions between them felt stilted and frightening.

Neither want to acknowledge their reactive aspects from old childhood wounds. In fact, both have disowned those parts of themselves that initially the other had found attractive. Max has disowned his own spontaneity, fear and neediness. Yvonne has disowned her anger and her desire to control. Remember, as I said earlier, the personality aspect we disown returns to us exactly as we disowned it, and the primary vehicle for this return is intimate relationships.

For example, since Yvonne couldn't tolerate her own feelings of anger, she acted in ways that stimulated Max's anger, which shifted the blame to him. Max found his own neediness and fear abhorrent, so he said things that triggered Yvonne's fear and neediness and then rejected her response. That's that tricky interaction called projective identification. I don't believe any of us interact that way consciously. But conscious or not, the only way to salvage their relationship is to put boundaries around reactivity to each other and begin to own their split-off parts. We need to remember that these reaction patterns come from un-metabolized emotional or physical trauma in childhood. If Yvonne understood where Max's need to control came from, perhaps she could respond with more intention and consistency when plans are made. If Max understood Yvonne's perspective, he could begin to hold Yvonne's love for him and resist reacting with such disappointment and anger. He needs to understand that his anger originates from growing up in a home where there was no chance for spontaneity or childlike behavior. Rosalie Jesse says that narcissistic injury inflicts hurt. The response to the hurt is fear or anxiety, the fear of annihilation or abandonment. The defense against the fear is anger and the way the person attempts to restore a sense of personal efficacy or effectiveness is to control.[4] Max's attachment pattern was anxious-avoidant which made him inaccessible. Yvonne, whose attachment was anxious, doesn't complain or say what she needs, and consequently she has so much abandonment despair that it is palpable.

It's imperative that Max and Yvonne discover the triggers for their anxiety, rage, shame and fear in their interactions. For some a trigger can be a suggestion that they hear as criticism. For others it may be feeling overwhelmed by intimacy. I have worked with couples for whom the triggers were a certain look or even a compliment. Clearly, for Max the primary

---

4. Rosalie C. Jesse, *Children in Recovery: Healing the Parent-Child Relationship in Alcoholic Addicted Families* (New York: Norton, 1989).

trigger was when plans were changed. For Yvonne the primary trigger was threat of abandonment. To avoid discharging these triggers, couples can avoid a bonding pattern problem by taking time out and returning to the conversation later when each may have more clarity, or by expressing the vulnerability that is masked by these bonding patterns. If Max could express his vulnerability instead of entering into his wounded ego state, it's possible for the discussion not to escalate into a painful struggle. By telling Yvonne how hurt he feels when she participates in this behavior, he defuses the negative bonding pattern. This allows an opportunity for Yvonne to become accountable for her behavior instead of being preoccupied with managing her anxiety.

Above all, it's up to each of us to practice containment and self-discipline. Reactivity in relationship is destructive and understanding the root of these responses is helpful. However, each person must choose to be conscious of their responses and body cues, to notice the tightening gut, the flushed face, the palpitating heart. Some of us know that this can happen as a result of something as simple as our partner asking if dinner is ready yet. Instead of unleashing our anger and fear on those we love, we need to train ourselves to take time out and discern to whom and to what we're responding. When difficult interactions occur, the couple may have to be very intentional about the way they process their emotions with each other. This may mean *doing what you are not inclined to do* and stretching into behavior that is foreign to you.[5] With that intentionality will come changed emotional habits and less conflict in relationships.

James Varigu, who is a pioneer in subpersonality theory, says, "We are responsible for our subpersonalities just as we're

---

5. Harville Hendrix, *Getting the Love You Want* (New York: Henry Holt, 1987).

responsible for our children, our pets and our car. We certainly need to see that they don't cause trouble to ourselves or to others." [6] In our relationships it's up to each of us to decide who is conducting our internal orchestra and which player is going to get the magic spotlight of our attention. It wouldn't be tolerable to see an angry two year old attempt to conduct "Swan Lake." It may be entertaining once, but if we have season tickets and made a commitment to go, it wouldn't be tolerated again. When we interact with others, we can be the conductor, or what Gregory Bateson calls the "witness." [7] This is the true self or the observing "I" who knows the value of each ego state and how they have served us. When conflict occurs, we can develop intra-personal boundaries and be aware when it's time to put our two year old to bed.

Suggestions for Unlocking Bonding Patterns

1. Become aware of our vulnerability and when hurt or fear is triggered.
2. Learn how to soothe ourselves and contain temporarily the vulnerability until it feels less loaded.
3. Learn to express that vulnerability honestly.
4. Pay attention to body cues to notice when a bonding pattern is becoming activated.
5. Learn when it's necessary to take time out and halt the interaction.
6. Learn to set boundaries with each other.
7. Learn to tolerate the in-betweeness or ambiguity.

---

6. James Varigu, *Psychosynthesis Workbook: Subpersonalities* (San Marcos, California: Synthesis, 1974).
7. Gregory Bateson, *Mind and Nature: Unnecessary Unity* (New York: Dutton, 1978).

Sometimes interactions can't be resolved after one attempt, and out of our own anxiety we provoke our partners to some conclusion that is laden with hurt or anger. After all, for many of us any conclusion is better than none! If we can allow ourselves to stay present through conflict with our vulnerability intact but contained, often we can reach a resolution that entails a true shift in consciousness. Our ability to sustain the tension of in-betweeness demands both a discipline of maintaining our intra-personal boundaries and surrender to the process of relinquishing the outcome to a greater good. Sometimes no amount of trying or technique can change a hideous interaction. When a couple is able to stand in the tension of struggle without reacting, a clarity of awareness can emerge.

Donna and Nancy have a relationship that is distinguished by years of reactivity and battle scars. Most of their battles are waged in the morning when Donna needs connection and Nancy is focused on trying to get ready for work. Nancy is often unresponsive to Donna's touch, and Donna often sets up a double bind by asking for touch when Nancy is preoccupied.

One morning, Donna went in to hug Nancy who was focused on getting dressed and Nancy dismissed her with a smile and a wave of the hand. Donna was hurt and stormed into the other room. Nancy knew from previous experience that if something wasn't done, the entire day and evening would be filled with tension. Nancy's typical reaction was to feel that she can never get it right, that she is not meant to be in a relationship and that she may as well give up. She'd sit and cry, or try to talk Donna out of her bad mood by rationalizing. Nancy had tried doing exercises that were empathic, but Donna wanted nothing to do with it. Eventually, they'd get into a horrible fight that would bleed on into the evening.

On this particular day Nancy made a deliberate choice not to react, but approached Donna and told her that she felt such despair at not giving her the response she needed. While she said this, Nancy noticed how overwhelmingly sad she felt, but chose to acknowledge it and go on. Donna seemed disgusted by yet another "lame excuse" by Nancy and told her that obviously she just didn't understand how hurtful it was to her. Instead of getting hysterical, Nancy stayed with her despair and also witnessed Donna's pain. Both of them stayed in the room and remained in uncomfortable silence while they became aware of their pain, their powerlessness and their overwhelming love for each other. Nancy took a good look at Donna's face, stood up and took Donna in her arms. As she held Donna, she stroked her hair and told her how much she cared about her. Donna dropped her defensiveness and surrendered to Nancy's embrace. Nancy's response was genuine and came not from fear, but from her true self, the part of her that is loving and knows what needs to be transcended in this situation. Nancy's willingness to stretch into new behavior, put boundaries around her own emotions, and stay in the moment of tension with her partner led to a shift in consciousness that inspired new behavior. She was able to maintain her courage and vulnerability in the midst of uncertainty.

Creating and healing boundaries is a challenging task for all of us. Certainly it's difficult enough to deal with the conscious aspects of this work, but when we recognize the even more complex inner dynamics, it will really demand courage and commitment. It's hard to give up our desire for magical healing, a desire based on the perception of a powerless child who has no other recourse. But our decision to react as adults, *not as children*, is exactly what will allow our relationships to thrive. No one can know or set our boundaries for us. This is the ultimate truth that cannot be avoided, but serenity is possible and the work has multiple rewards.

CHAPTER 12

Relationships: The Most Rigorous Spiritual Path

"Whatever we disown,
life brings back to us exactly
as we have disowned it!"

Sheldon Kopp

T here's a saying that love brings out anything unlike itself, and the more illuminating the love is, the darker our shadows appear. The path of relationship allows us to become aware of those parts of ourselves that keep us from being whole. The I Ching advises, "Adverse relationships provide opportunity for inner growth and development as we overcome the doubts, anxieties and judgments that block our access to the Creative Power."[1] True soul work begins when we draw on those dark places deep inside and step into the mystery of loving.

Through intimacy we reflect everything that exists within us . . . our wounded child, our divine child, our narcissism, our shame and even our patterns of attachment. All that has

---

1. Carol Anthony, *Coming to Meet: Advice from the I Ching,* Excerpt from "Larger Visions of Relationship" (Stow, Massachusetts: Anthony, 1988), 245.

been hidden from us is revealed through love. Sheldon Kopp says that whatever we had to hide from mother or father's disapproving eyes, became hidden and then unseen by our own.[2] When we give ourselves to relationship, unconsciously we take all of our unfinished business and we give it to our partners. Whatever attachment pattern we've developed in childhood, we will repeat unless we do our work.

The synchronicity of all this is astounding! Lets say you were raised with smothering, engulfing parents. Sure enough, you will turn on your radar and unconsciously go scouting . . . some enchanted evening across a crowded workshop . . . you will be attracted to that man or woman who likes to control. Or, were you raised in a disengaged family with parents who abandoned you or couldn't sustain closeness? Sure enough, you will feel drawn to that individual who can't sustain intimacy and may abandon you. Obviously, doing this dance of intimacy is filled with potential for growth. But if our wounded child is leading the dance, we don't learn our lessons. Since we teach what we need to learn, I will give you an example from my own relational past.

There was a long time in my childhood where I felt I could do nothing right. The feeling was magnified at school where I felt incompetent, discouraged and very angry. I wanted to forget that part of my history, and I succeeded fairly well until I gave this piece of "unfinished business" to my partner. The scene went something like this: I was frying eggs one Sunday morning. Everything was going fine until my husband came into the kitchen and said, "Dear, don't you think you should turn those eggs over?"

My blood pressure soared. I slammed down the spatula and

---

2. Sheldon Kopp, *Even a Stone Can Be a Teacher: Learning and Growing from the Experiences of Everyday Life* (Los Angeles: Jeremy Tarcher, 1985).

yelled, "Don't you think I can handle cooking eggs after 10 years! Are you so bored that you have nothing else to do? Why don't you get the hell out of this kitchen and occupy yourself for awhile and leave me alone!"

He did just that, and the rest of the day was spent in cold, stony silence. The truth is that his comment felt like a criticism, and literally I tumbled back into the emotions of the child who couldn't seem to do anything right. Ironically, the rest of the day with my husband I couldn't do anything right either, so I got to relive that memory. During those years of marriage, I had very little notion of an emotional comfort zone and felt unable to control my reactions.

John Welwood says that "at some point the person you love, becomes the person you choose to see as your worst enemy." [3] Have you ever noticed that sometimes we treat our lovers or partners worse than anyone else? I have to say, I wouldn't treat a friend like I treated my husband that morning. I wouldn't even treat a stranger like that! *The more intimate a relationship becomes, the more infantile and punitive our models of relating get, because intimacy strikes at our vulnerable core.* When we were children, every myth, every movie and every romance story taught us that we were promised the ideal lover. So what happened!?

It's bizarre, but we do indeed find that person. Once I attended a workshop that examined the spirituality of relationships and the gifts our partners bring to us in the form of lessons. It struck me as odd when the instructor referred to his wife as his "beloved teacher," a term that catapulted me into a perspective that has been useful for me in helping other couples. His term impressed me so much that it serves as a

---

3. John Welwood, *Conscious Relationships* (Boulder, Colorado: Sounds True Recording, 1993).

reminder to this day that we attract *exactly* the right individuals, those who will bring our shadows into the light.

As adults, we tend to pick people for relationship who have opposite attachment styles but *complementary wounds.* Let's say you have an anxious attachment history and you are attracted to a person who appears calm, reliable and in control. As life goes on, you find that he is so calm, that sometimes you have to hold a mirror under his nose to be sure he's breathing! His control turns to anger and you become anxious because he pushes you away. Ah yes! Captain Karma is at work again! You have wound up with a guy who has an avoidant attachment history! He may have the same abandonment issues as you do, but his style is just a little different and strangely resembles one of your primary caregivers. How very odd! As you read further in this book, you will find that this situation is common in virtually all intimate relationships. It is precisely when these patterns become visible that couples get discouraged and want to give up. The real soul work begins when intimacy illumines these dark places and we take a hard look at the ways we are defended against love.

In adulthood we re-enact our childhood events, and intimacy is the vehicle that allows us to look at those wounded aspects of ourselves that still need to be healed. It's absolutely true that we can't see our own image without a mirror and being our mirror is the gift that relationship brings. If we want relationships that are whole and dynamic, then we will allow our love and vulnerability to take us deep inside our souls and emerge with a more expansive view of ourselves. If we resist or lack the courage to do this kind of inner exploration, then healthy intimacy will remain unknown to us. Lacking this type of self exploration, many of us will go from one painful relationship to another looking for what inevitably we must give ourselves.

Relational Re-enactment

You don't have to grow up in an unhealthy family environment to experience relational re-enactment. Lucky us; even adults from the healthiest families get to relive the past through relationship. Since none of us had perfect parents, we all come into adulthood with unmet needs and unresolved pain. In personal and professional relationships we re-enact our childhood events through dependency, distortion, provocation and selection. Let's examine those dynamics that propel us to learn our lessons.

Dependency

Dependent relationships occur when our desire and hunger for attachment is so strong that it overrides our ability to act in our own best interest. Another way to describe it is that when I get involved with you, it's not out of conscious choice, but unmet childhood needs. The classic book by Robin Norwood, *Women Who Love Too Much*, could easily be renamed "Girls and Boys Who Weren't Loved Enough"! Anyone who has ever been in a dependent relationship knows how magical and seductive it feels . . . at first. As the mist of romance starts to clear, we find out how destructive, manipulative and painful dependency is. When we have denied gaping childhood wounds, we'll get into a relationship and ultimately create a dysfunctional mom or dad out of our partners. Of course, it's not that we create this by ourselves. We have to have a willing partner who will participate!

There are reasons why we become attracted to the same type of person again and again. They may come in different shapes, sizes and packaging so we think this time it will be different. But when the veneer is peeled away, we'll have someone with the correct "wiring" to relive the dance of dependency. Remember, we pick people with complementary wounds. Just because a lover appears to be independent and self-sufficient doesn't mean that he or she don't have similar dependency needs. The attachment style could be the opposite of yours, but the core needs will be the same. Sometimes people appear to be *counter-dependent*, which means that they resist their "distasteful, offensive" urge for dependency, by acting extremely independent. Consequently, often one person in the relationship will carry the shame of being childlike and needy. However, it takes two people with dependency issues to relive this pattern.

For people who identify with this style of relating, the revolving door of dependent relationships can stop when we take time to sort out our childhood patterns of attachment. This may mean calling a temporary timeout in relationships to examine our boundary patterns and meet face to face our demons of despair, emptiness and desperate longing. Scary as that sounds, there's a precious gift waiting on the other side which is the knowledge that we no longer have to depend on others to fill our emptiness. During this timeout it's possible to learn how to soothe ourselves through meditation, movement, music, yoga or even talking to a friend.

It will be extremely helpful during this time to work with a guide who can take us through our inner wilderness. In fact, for we who are in early recovery from childhood trauma or addiction, it's imperative that we consult with our therapist or sponsor before making any sudden changes in our relational life. I'm not suggesting that we go into isolation and call a halt to all relationships. We mustn't abandon our children, jobs or friends. This isn't punishment for bad behavior! Rather, it's a time to create our own sacred space, a comfort zone that will allow us to relate from a place of empowerment, not neediness.

Distortion

The process of distortion is unconscious and certainly not intentional. Our minds will go to any length to keep us from our pain and distortion is one means we use to avoid dealing with the past. Working with couples has allowed me to witness the raging conflict that sometimes leads to the demise of the relationship. This conflict can be triggered by a helpful suggestion, a glance, forgetting to buy milk at the grocery or even a compliment! When David, for example, rages at his wife because dinner is ten minutes late, you can bet that it's based on old agenda.

Distortion means that we distort our view of a current person or a situation that correlates directly with a person or a situation in our past. Distortion is so tricky because unconsciously we're always on guard so nothing contradicts what we need to go on believing. When distortion occurs, I *need* to see my husband as the bastard or the hero because if I really dug into the source of my hurt and rage I may have to look at my own father. That would be too painful and it would feel too disloyal to contradict my family rules. So it's more convenient to distort my view of my husband instead. Distortion means that we won't allow ourselves to see clearly who's in front of us or the real source of our pain. Instead, we're flipped back to the past where anger, forgetfulness, unpredictability or even dinner time has loaded meaning for us. When someone trips this live wire, we get carried away by emotional reaction. We slip out of focus into almost an emotional memory state where reason doesn't function. Is this a result of growing up in a dysfunctional family? Not necessarily, although abuse, abandonment and enmeshment certainly intensifies this dynamic. Distortion is a universal dynamic and it serves to remind us of those wounds that keep us from being whole.

The antidote for distortion is to learn where our reactivity triggers are located and how to calm ourselves down. Unfortunately, the drug of choice for some of us is adrenaline, and conflict certainly gets our blood flowing, although not necessarily to the brain. When intimacy becomes confused with intensity, we lose self-discipline and indulge ourselves in arrogance. We dive into interactions that we know are sensitive and proceed with little forethought. We walk right into the fire assuming that this time we can fix it.

Our bodies always give us warning clues when we are about to distort an interaction. For example, if you come home hungry and tired and find that dinner isn't prepared, maybe your gut tightens and your face gets hot. That's the time to think before you say or do anything. Or perhaps your partner gives you "that look" when he asks sweetly if you deposited the rent check. You feel your teeth clench and your head start to throb. *That's* reaction and warning, and that's the time to pause and say "Excuse me for a minute." Then leave the room temporarily, to calm down and move into an emotional boundary that will work for you. Find a quiet place, take several deep breaths and use this affirmation:

> I can express my feelings about any person, any interaction or any situation. And I also acknowledge that the interpretations I give events may be more about my own personal history than what is going on right now.

Provocation

Provocation and distortion are two sides of the same coin. The end results are the same. Through distortion, we are triggered by situations that remind us of our past. Through provocation, we *create* situations or reactions that are similar to our past. Examples of provocation are plentiful and often funny, unless we are living out the dynamic.

Some time ago, I worked with Anna and George, an intelligent couple that had difficulty in their relationship. Even though Anna was raised by a critical father, she married a man who wasn't particularly critical. Still, conflict reigned in this relationship and this couple didn't have a clue why their interactions almost always escalated into a fight. One day George arrived on time for a therapy appointment, and we began the weekly ritual of waiting for Anna. It was clear that George hated waiting for anyone, and his impatience was palpable. After ten minutes of waiting, Anna rushed in the door and threw herself into a chair.

"You don't like my hair, do you?" she said to George. Amazed, he said he hadn't said a thing about her hair. "You don't *have* to say anything. You always look at me like that when you don't like how I look!"

Then he got angry and reminded her that he had been waiting for ten minutes, their appointment was costing money and they should stop wasting time! Nonetheless, she continued to badger him relentlessly about her hair. By the end of the encounter, he didn't like her or her hair.

That's provocation. When we use provocation, literally we incite the kinds of responses similar to those we received from our caregivers. Again, it isn't done with forethought or malice, and usually not even with conscious awareness. By the way, those who use this dynamic do not just limit it to lovers. We provoke friends, supervisors, our children and even innocent bystanders like waiters, clerks or flight attendants!

Years ago, I dined periodically with my friend Sara who constantly got into conflict with waiters or waitresses who seemed incompetent. It's not that she complained politely if the portions were small. She became enraged that they brought a meal that wasn't prepared to her satisfaction! Her daughter got so embarrassed that she kicked her mother under the table!

Now, when she looks back, she remembers her feelings of bitter disappointment combined with anger that welled up inside of her when the food wasn't prepared the way she wanted it. Her reaction was overwhelming and inappropriate to the circumstances. As we talked, she remembered that as a child she loved to eat and she was also overweight, so she couldn't eat what or as much as she wanted. She remembered, as a child, sitting at the dinner table feeling out of control, angry and disappointed. Her mother's reaction was usually irritation and finally anger. As an adult, Sarah unconsciously provoked similar responses in the people who were serving her dinner! Years later, she remarked how she could turn the most charming waiter into Attila the Hun!

To avoid provocation we must use the similar strategies that were suggested for the dynamic of distortion. When emotions become overwhelming and our bodies start to tense, it's time to practice containment. The first step is always to step into our comfort zone and do whatever we must to calm down. One suggestion for containing provocation is to talk about what we're experiencing with no blame or judgment. If Anna could have realized that she was angry before she walked into the therapy session, she could sit down and talk about how agitated she felt. For example, "I don't know why, but the closer I got to this therapy session, the more angry I felt." No blame and no judgment. "I love you more than I've ever loved anybody, and it scares me to death and sometimes I know I push you away." Or, "I feel vulnerable tonight and I know I have a short fuse, would you order dinner for me while I make a phone call?" It takes courage to be honest about our vulnerability, but doing so will diffuse overwhelming emotions that lead to provocation.

Selection

"I want a girl, just like the girl that married dear old Dad!" Whether we agree or are nauseated by the lyrics of that song, the choices we make in relationship usually aren't accidental. Selection is a common process by which we select or fall in love with people who have traits similar to our parents or significant people in our lives. All of us do it to some extent. It's part of being human.

However, there is no mistake. The choices we make in relationship aren't accidental. That's why daughters of alcoholics tend to marry alcoholics, why daughters of spouse abusers are six times more likely to marry men who abuse them, why sons who witness spouse battering are four times more likely to abuse their wives. Are we nuts? No. It's not about being crazy, but about how our spirit propels us into situations where we can take a closer look at what stands in the way of our ability to experience love. Whatever we have disowned, life will bring back to us exactly as we have disowned it until we learn the lesson it has to teach.

In workshops I do an exercise with the audience that allows them to become aware of the specific similarities between their caregivers and their mates. When the realization hits, I hear either groans or laughter, depending on the status of their current relationship and the work they have done on themselves. Inevitably, there are questions from discouraged participants, wondering if they have to find a new partner in order to make better choices. I tell them of course not! In fact, I congratulate them for finding someone with whom they can heal.

The truth is, if you've found someone who has similar negative and positive characteristics as your caregivers, potentially it's a very powerful match! Those who have read Harville Hendrix' work on *Imago Therapy* will understand how healing this type of relationship can be. However, both people in the relationship must be willing to work if they are to become aware of the factors that brought them together and what history keeps them from loving fully.

Knowing about the selection process helps us to be conscious and take responsibility for our choices. It's always a temptation to blame our partners for relationship failures. We rationalize that "if he weren't so tight with money, or if he wasn't such a slob," we could be happier! While that may be true, we need to take a look at the role we play in relationship and the reasons we chose each other in the first place. When we blame others, we end our responsibility there. Family therapist Murray Bowen said that the extent to which we blame others is the extent to which emotionally we are stuck in our family of origin.[4]

That doesn't mean if you are in an abusive, violent relationship that you have to ignore the violence and take on the burden of responsibility. When it comes to abuse, we can't turn the other cheek and spiritualize our problems! On the contrary, creating safety for ourselves by establishing our boundaries has to be our top priority. When delving into our relationship patterns we must have one foot in the here and now and one foot grounded in our spirituality. One of my mentors said that if we spiritualize our problems, we are literally no earthly good!

When we're involved in painful relationships, it's hard to realize value in any of our pain. But, remember that all detours are valuable. It takes time to gain insight from our experience. Indulging ourselves in self criticism is detrimental to our soul and keeps us rigidly entrenched in our suffering.

---

4. Murray Bowen, *Family Therapy in Clinical Practice* (Northvale, New Jersey: James Aronson, 1978).

Creating a comfort zone means that we can cease the habit of reaction that prevents us from learning the priceless wisdom of our lessons. I've given you suggestions in this chapter that will help you create boundaries that will enhance your sense of self. But it's up to you to take those suggestions and do the work. No one can do it for you. Every spiritual path requires discipline, and the relationship path is no different. In order to prevent our past from destroying our well-being, we need to practice the art of relationship as we would practice yoga or meditation. When we really put our desires into action, the results will breathe healing into all of our interactions.

CHAPTER 13

Heart and Soul: Love's True Journey

"Death through love is life.
Whoever does not die of his love,
is unable to live by it. "

Sufi Proverb

The power of love allows us to bring light into the dark places of our soul. Falling in love inspires us to make the journey. Romantic love is that sense of synchronicity, that beautiful, symbiotic stage where our beloved seems a mirror of ourselves. We might say, as others have, "I can't believe we were both thinking of each other at 12:05 P.M.!" or, "We both love the same mouthwash, it's so incredible!" We feel an excitement in our hearts that at last we've found someone we can meld with. It's that wonderful, blissful experience we've read about and seen in movies since we were young.

In fairy tales, the princess is rescued by the prince from her (clinically interesting) family. The story always ends "happily ever after," so we never find out what happens when Cinderella wakes at 2:00 A.M. to a screaming baby and wishes that she had left Prince Charming to her stepsisters! Nor do we get to see what becomes of Snow White after one year of marriage, when all her abandonment issues are surfacing. In other words, we haven't had the opportunity to see how to handle our relationships when the real soul work begins!

Is it any wonder that we begin relationships and then leave when love starts illuminating those dark places? When our old childhood themes rise to be healed, some of the axioms we've heard over the years just don't ring true. For example, love does mean "letting go of fear," eventually. But it's more accurate to say that love means walking *into* fear, and we hope out the other side! And whoever believes that love means never having to say I'm sorry probably is no longer in relationship!

Actually, it's a good thing that we've read these stories and we have the ideal of romance. Otherwise, few of us would choose consciously to take this rigorous spiritual path.

Before we fall in love, our comfort zone is like a one-room apartment that is fashioned out of the limited views we have of ourselves and the survival strategies that have kept us in the illusion of safety. Of course, our one room is part of a larger mansion that we don't use and visit rarely. Then at some point the one room begins to feel claustrophobic and we feel isolated, lonely and not very alive. This is our soul that is pushing us to grow and expand. We figure that the answer is to bring someone into our lives, so we turn on our radar and go scouting for someone to love.

Miracle of miracles, we fall in love and find bliss, intoxication, gratitude and we get a glimpse of all the potential we hadn't realized. We've become pretty attached to our limited space and we start to feel some reluctance to expand outward. After all, it was long ago that we shut off the lights and locked the doors of the other rooms in our mansion. In fact, we may have even lost awareness that these rooms exist. But to make room for another we have to move out of our one-room apartment, and then we start to discover what else is there. As we begin to expand, we find that these rooms are dark and dusty from disuse and we're afraid to see what's in there—those disowned parts of ourselves that through love we will come to know. Lets say that as children we coped with loneliness by denying our need for love. We locked the door to loneliness and found safety in that single room. But when we fall in love and allow ourselves to be vulnerable, we can't avoid feeling again that desperate need for love. We entertain questions that feel life-threatening, like "What will happen if I need too much?" or "Will he/she go away and leave me?" We had a comfortable identity and now we've gone and fallen in love. Our identity has become so indistinct that we're scared, and we feel an overwhelming urge to run to our room and slam the door before we lose it altogether.

A Sufi poet said, *"Death through love is life. I give thanks to my beloved that she has held this out for me. Whoever does not die of his love, is unable to live by it."* When we come into our darkness through the light of love, we are faced with a choice. If we retreat to the confines of our room, everything will be familiar and safe. But if we want to grow, we must commit to a journey. At the crossroads of this decision is usually where most relationships collapse.

It's useful to understand that falling in love opens our hearts, but loving deeply touches our souls. Both aspects are important in relationship, but they serve different purposes. A heart connection is that feeling of openness and attraction we feel towards others. It can occur when we're crossing a street, looking across a room, or gazing into the eyes of our lover. When we open our hearts, it's a warm, sweet and inspiring experience and we are crazy about that someone just the way she or he is. This kind of opening is the stimulus to expand out of our one-room apartment and explore the rest of our internal home.

Then comes the soul connection. That attraction to others, not just because they make us feel good, but because there is a knowing that they will also make us expand and grow.[1] So, overtly we fall in love because our heart is open to another and it feels wonderful. The soul is attracted to someone who, as a French writer says, "will make us live and die most intensely." John Welwood says, "We begin to love [others] for all that they could be, as well as the sense that we have some role in their unfolding potential."[2]

After we are blessed with the experience of falling in love, the soul work of relationship really starts. When our beloved take us to those places of fear, anger and vulnerability, it takes all the courage and persistence we can muster to maintain our equilibrium. We wonder how such lovely romance could have turned into such bitter conflict? Please remember that the greater the attraction between individuals, the greater the potential for healing. However, the greater the attraction between individuals, the greater the potential for conflict. Conflict that occurs repeatedly about the same issue is not about the present, it's about the past.[3] I can tell you from experience that when the boat gets into stormy waters, there is a strong tendency to jump! Sometimes, it's a wise, lifesaving move to exit. But too often we choose to leave because it's just too frightening to unlock those parts of ourselves that remind us of our past. For those who are attempting to create or maintain our comfort zone in relationship, there is some cross-cultural wisdom that may help. Zulu people say that to

---

1. John Welwood, *Journey of the Heart: Intimate Relationships and the Path of Love* (New York: HarperCollins, 1990).

2. John Welwood, *Conscious Relationships* (Boulder, Colorado: Sounds True Recording, 1993).

3. Pat Love, *Understanding and Improving Love Relationships Through Imago Therapy* (Austin, Texas: Audio Presentation, 1993).

be fully alive, we must approach life with our "three faces" intact: the face of the child, the face of the young maiden or lad, and the face of the wise one.

The *face of the child* is that part of us that sees with fresh eyes and is aware of the wonder and magic in the world. It is the face that is still open to glorious possibilities.

The *face of the young lad or maiden* is that part of us that is consumed with our bodies, with our sensuality and with the fire of passion and discovery.

The *face of the wise one* is the gentle strength and wisdom that comes with age and insight. It is the face that has been etched with its journey.

To do the soul work needed to create well-being in all of our relationships, we need to carry all three faces with us. Sometimes it takes the eyes of the child or the wisdom of benign strength to see our relationships in perspective. Zulu people say that when we lose the ability to carry one of these faces, we start to walk the procession of the living dead.

Relationships give us an opportunity to grow into our potential. I know as well as you that when we're in a painful situation, that's little comfort. I would never advocate remaining in an abusive situation, but some people have such damaged boundaries that they haven't a clue whether their relationship is violent, or if it's just within a normal range of stress. If we want to access our wisdom and discern what actions will serve us best, here are some suggestions that will help sustain our comfort zones while we do the soul work required for growth: [4]

---

4. This material is included in A. Arriens research which she has amplified and expanded into her educational training, *The Four Fold Way* (New York: HarperCollins, 1993). For use of this material you must receive permission from the office of A. Arrien, P.O. Box 2077, Sausalito, CA 94966, 415-331-5050. All materials are copyrighted.

Show up! Not just physically, but in heart and mind and
spirit. If we are to heal our boundaries, we must be present and fully conscious. If you can't be fully present
then say so! There is nothing more painful than trying
to communicate with someone whose feet are firmly
planted in the air. If you find yourself spacing out, take
some time to breathe, step into your boundaries and
return to the interaction.

Pay attention to what has heart meaning. It keeps us vital
and alive in our soul work. We need to pay close attention to the times when we feel half-hearted, weak-hearted,
open-hearted or closed-hearted. If you are in a relationship feeling *half-hearted*, then perhaps the timing is not
right to do the work that is required. If you are feeling
weak-hearted in a relationship, this often means that you
lack the courage to say what is true. Many individuals
become numb and deadened, because they have *closed*
their hearts to their partners. When this occurs, we not
only damage our soul, but we begin to see the whole
world in shades of gray instead of brilliant color. This is
the time that many choose to have affairs or flirtations
just to jump-start their vitality and passion.

To open our hearts again is literally a life-saving endeavor.
To do this, we need to remember what in our life inspires
us, what touches or delights us, and where we feel challenged. When we open our hearts again, we can discern
what has meaning for us and create a sense of well-being
wherever we are.

Tell the truth without blame or judgment. To avoid reactivity and de-escalate conflict, we can learn to comment
on our reality without the harsh blade of judgment. This
may mean that we have to discipline ourselves to step
into our emotional boundary and do what is necessary to
calm down. When we are angry, scared or hurt, we tend

to attack or bypass our emotions. Rather we can say, "I am so angry right now that I want to hurt you, so I'm going to take some time to cool off." Or, "When you pay more attention to other women I feel insecure. I am not asking you to pay full attention to me all the time, but I would like you to acknowledge my presence when I am with you." These are courageous statements that allow us to go deeper into ourselves and deepen the bonds of intimacy.

Be open to outcome rather than fixated on outcome. Letting go isn't an easy skill for anyone. However, when we are open to outcome, it expands our possibilities of being. Rather than, "this relationship has to look this way!" we can bring forward the face of the child who says, "I wonder what we will create together?" When we are not so fixated on the outcome, our inner wisdom and objectivity is more available to us. To be open to outcome, we need to practice detachment in all of our relationships. This doesn't mean that we become disinterested and complacent, it means that we learn to care deeply from a place of perspective. Harrison Owens created the four "immutable laws" of detachment which can help us in all relationships: [5]

1. When it begins, it is always the right time.
2. Whoever shows up, is exactly the right person.
3. Whatever happens, is the only thing that could have happened.
4. When it's over . . . it's over!

---

5. Harrison Owens, *Leadership Is* (Potomac, Maryland: Abbott, 1990).

If we can identify a challenging or inspiring relationship in our lives, it's not hard to see how these principles can enhance our well-being. Practicing detachment is the knowing that whenever the relationship began was exactly the perfect time for it to begin. Thus, we may as well give up cursing ourselves and ruminating about how we could have avoided this relationship, because the timing was, in some way, perfect for our growth.

Whoever showed up was exactly the right person at that time. If we complain that his or her hair was the wrong color, or we didn't see how lazy he or she was, we might as well let it go! In hindsight you will discover that the timing and the person was absolutely right for you to do your work. Whatever has transpired in the relationship was the only thing that could have happened. Therefore, with objectivity and wisdom, we will come to realize that psychologically, intellectually and spiritually, each person was acting or reacting in the only way that they could have at the time. No doubt the lessons we've learned have been valuable. If we've gained insight from the experiences, the lessons won't have to be repeated, or at least they won't have to be so painful.

Finally, we may be preoccupied with particular aspects of our relationship that are different now, or even gone. The first kiss, the first time our eyes met, the night we spent hours talking and never went to sleep are precious moments that can be re-kindled, but they'll never be quite the same. When we are obsessed with what was instead of what is, there's no way for the relationship to grow and we sentence ourselves to misery. It's as if we shut ourselves up in that one-room apartment again and are willing to live in perpetual grief. In fact, if a relationship doesn't grow out of the romantic stage into differentiation, what happens inevitably is a hostile/dependent relationship.

That doesn't mean that romance can't continue. It does

mean that as the relationship deepens, the romance will also deepen and change form. For example, I know a woman who has done the work of repairing her emotional boundaries, but there are times when she deeply mourns the raging fights and the wonderful make up sessions. For this couple, fighting was their only way to express passion and now they need to find new ways to create fire between them. When we detach from what was, we can acknowledge that whatever part of the relationship is over, is over! That acknowledgement brings release and an atmosphere in which new expressions of intimacy can blossom.

Within each one of us is the ability to create the quality of life we desire. We must find the courage to move beyond the pain, violence and deprivation of the past, into lives that bring us the gifts of well-being and comfort. We must do this, not just for ourselves, but for the survival of Mother Earth. *The chaos and violence in the world is a macrocosm of what is going on between people.*

Creating a comfort zone is establishing an internal sacred space where we can respond to each other with integrity and not with ancient, outworn patterns that don't serve us well. Allowing ourselves to explore consciously the heart and soul of relationship is how we enter this state of grace. When finally we emerge from our one-room apartments and embrace the totality of who we are, we will carry with us a sanctuary of peace wherever we go.

We don't have to travel to Tibet or search out gurus to find this sense of sanctuary. We don't have to buy the latest model of car or take drugs to be acceptable. Life in the comfort zone allows us to be in relationships with the quiet, confident knowing of who we are. It is also the sacred container that holds the vision of who we can become.

APPENDIX

Declaration of Interdependence

We human beings are not solitary creatures, we have powerful needs for affiliation and belonging. Recognizing this, we commit ourselves to cultivate a sense of community. This means that we will set goals and work together to accomplish those goals that inspire the highest potential in all human beings. We will encourage freedom, protection and right use of power so that all individuals can use their creativity and wisdom to fulfill a higher purpose: to make our world a better place to live.

Through the course of our lives we have demonstrated that our actions have impact that reaches far beyond ourselves. We realize that we will benefit individually by contributing to the quality of life in our communities and in our world.

We value diversity and are aware of the richness this brings to our lives. Moreover, we have a responsibility to encourage all people to join us in this effort, regardless of race, gender, sexual preference, age, beliefs or personal appearance.

We are willing to share our successes and failure, our hopes and fears, and our joys and sorrows with others in our life. Our ability to instill a clear sense of interdependence is dependent on our efforts to communicate clearly, honestly and compassionately.

Conducting our lives with conscience and dignity, we will not stand by and tolerate violations to ourselves or those around us. We honor the sacredness in all living things, and we are mindful of this in all our relationships, including our relationship with Mother Earth.

BIBLIOGRAPHY

Ainsworth, Mary, et. al. *Patterns of Attachment.* Hillsdale, N.J.: Erlbaum, 1978.

Anthony, Carol. *Coming to Meet: Advice from the I Ching.* Stow: Massachusetts, 1988.

Arrien, Angeles. *The Four-Fold Way: Walking the Paths of the Warrior, Teacher, Healer and Visionary.* New York: HarperCollins, 1993.

Bandler, Richard. *Using Your Brain for a Change.* Moab, Utah: Real People Press, 1985.

Bandler, Richard and John Grinder. *Reframing: Neuro-Linguistic Programming and the Transformation of Meaning.* Moab, Utah: Real People Press, 1982.

Barker, Raymond Charles. *The Power of Decision.* New York: Perigree Books, 1991.

189

Berenson, David and E.W. Schrier. "Family Dynamics in Addressing Denial in the Therapy of Alcohol Problems." *Family Dynamics of Addiction Quarterly*, December 1991.

Boszormenyi-Nagy, Ivan and Geraldine M. Spark. *Invisible Loyalties*. New York: Harper & Row, 1973.

Bowen, Murray. *Family Therapy in Clinical Practice*. Northvale, N.J.: James Aronson, 1978.

Buber, Martin. *I and Thou*. New York: Scribner, 1978.

Fossom, Merle and Marilyn Mason. *Facing Shame, Families in Recovery*. New York: Norton, 1993.

Grof, Christina and Stanislav Grof. *Spiritual Emergency: When Personal Transformation Becomes a Crisis*. Los Angeles: Jeremy Tarcher, 1989.

Hendrix, Harville. *Getting the Love You Want*. New York: Henry Holt, 1987.

Huxley, Aldus. *Brave New World*. New York: HarperCollins, 1932.

Jesse, Rosalie C. *Children in Recovery: Healing the Parent-Child Relationship in Alcohol-Addicted Families*. New York: Norton, 1989.

Karen, Robert. "Becoming Attached." *Atlantic Monthly*, February 1990.

Keleman, Stanley. *Somatic Reality*. Berkeley: Center Press, 1979.

_____. *Your Body Speaks Its Mind*. Berkeley: Center Press, 1981.

Kopp, Sheldon. *Even a Stone Can Be a Teacher: Learning and Growing from the Experiences of Everyday Life*. Los Angeles: Jeremy Tarcher, 1985.

Levin, Pamela. *Cycles of Power*. Deerfield Beach, Florida: Health Communications, Inc., 1988.

Main, Mary. "Becoming Attached," Atlantic Monthly, February 1990.

Miller, Alice. *Drama of the Gifted Child*. New York: Basic Books, 1994.

Millman, Dan. *The Life You Were Born to Live*. Tiburon, California: H.J. Kramer, Inc., 1993.

Olson, David. *The Circumplex Model*. New York: Haworth Press, 1989.

Orwell, George. *1984*. New York: NAL-Dutton, 1950.

Owens, Harrison. *Leadership Is*. Potomac, Maryland: Abbot, 1990.

Peterson, Marilyn. *At Personal Risk*. New York: Norton , 1992.

Putnam, Frank. *Diagnosis and Treatment of Multiple Personality Disorder*. New York: Guilford Press, 1989.

Rowan, John. *Subpersonalities: The People Inside Us*. New York: Routledge, 1990.

Varigu, James. *Psychosynthesis Workbook: Subpersonalities*. San Marcos, California: Synthesis, 1974.

Watzlavick, Paul and Charles E. Weakland. Change: *Principles of Problem Formation and Problem Resolution*. New York: Norton, 1974.

Welwood, John. *Journey of the Heart: Intimate Relationships and the Path of Love*. New York: HarperCollins, 1990.

Winnicott, D.W. *Talking to Parents*. Reading, Massachusetts: Addison-Wesley, 1994.

Zinker, Joseph. *In Search of Good Form: Gestalt Therapy with Couples and Family*. San Francisco: Jossey-Bass, 1994.

ABOUT THE AUTHOR

Rokelle Lerner is one of the most sought after speakers and trainers on relationships, women's issues and addicted family systems. She has inspired audiences throughout the world with her expertise and her ability to address difficult topics with insight, humor and astounding clarity.

She has received numerous awards for her work with children and families including *Esquire* magazine's "Top 100 Women in the U.S. Who Are Changing the Nation." Rokelle has consulted with foreign governments, U.S. agencies, corporations, schools and hundreds of individuals on boundaries, addiction and relationship problems. Rokelle has appeared as a guest consultant on many television shows such as *Oprah, Good Morning America, CBS Morning News* and *20/20*. Her articles and interviews have been featured in the *Washington Post, New York Times, Los Angeles Times, Newsweek, Time, People Magazine* and *Parents Magazine*.

She is the author of the bestselling books *Affirmations for*

Adult Children of Alcoholics and *Affirmations for the Inner Child*. Rokelle has also produced several bestselling audiocassettes including *From Victimization to Empowerment, Boundaries and Relationships, Craving Love—Afraid to Love, The Challenge of Intimacy* and *The Quest for Wholeness*.

In addition to her speaking schedule, Rokelle conducts three- to five-day intensive seminars on boundaries and the spirituality of relationships in locations throughout the country. For further information on her couples seminar, women's retreats or training for therapists, or to contact her for a presentation, please write or call:

Rokelle Lerner & Associates
420 Summit Ave., Suite 28
St. Paul, MN 55102
(612) 227-4031

Famous Women Discuss Their Spiritual Experiences

Embracing Our Essence
Spiritual Conversations with Prominent Women
Susan Skog

In the first shining collection of its kind, 29 prominent women of our time intimately share with you the philosophies, practices, touchstones and struggles that shape their lush interiors. They discuss the source of the pulsing spirituality sweeping our country and why it's our only hope for personal fulfillment and evolution as a society. The powerful messages shared in this book invite women to discover their own spiritual essence: the intuitiveness, wisdom and compassion that have the power to transform the world. *Embracing Our Essence* is also valuable solace to women and men discovering their own spiritual strength.

Code 3596 paperback **$11.95**
Code 3782 hardcover. **$22.00**

*Available at your favorite bookstore or call
1-800-441-5569 for Visa or MasterCard orders.
Prices do not include shipping and handling.
Your response code is HCI.*

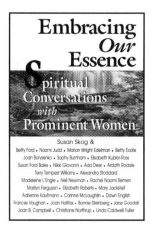

Susan Skog &
Betty Ford • Naomi Judd • Marian Wright Edelman • Betty Eadie
Joan Borysenko • Sophy Burnham • Elisabeth Kubler-Ross
Susan Ford Bales • Nikki Giovanni • Ada Deer • Ardath Rodale
Terry Tempest Williams • Alexandra Stoddard
Madeleine L'Engle • Nell Newman • Rachel Naomi Remen
Marilyn Ferguson • Elizabeth Roberts • Mary Jacksteit
Adrienne Kaufmann • Corinne McLaughlin • Dawn English
Frances Vaughan • Joan Halifax • Bonnie Steinberg • Jane Goodall
Joan B. Campbell • Christiane Northrup • Linda Caldwell Fuller

Includes interviews with:

Betty Ford
Naomi Judd
Marian Wright Edelman
Betty Eadie
Joan Borysenko
Sophy Burnham
Elisabeth Kubler-Ross
Susan Ford Bales
Nikki Giovanni
Ada Deer
Ardath Rodale
Jane Goodall
Linda Caldwell Fuller
Terry Tempest Williams
Alexandra Stoddard
Madeleine L 'Engle
Nell Newman
Rachel Naomi Remen
Marilyn Ferguson
Elizabeth Roberts
Mary Jacksteit
Adrienne Kaufmann
Corinne McLaughlin
Dawn English
Frances Vaughan
Joan Halifax
Bonnie Steinberg
Joan B. Campbell
Christiane Northrup

Join Us for an
Embracing Our Essence Gathering

On this very special long weekend in spring 1996, we'll explore our spiritual strength together. Many of the women from the book, along with other high profile women, will lead thought-provoking spiritual presentations and discussion workshops. It's an experience you'll long remember. Call 1-800-441-5569 for details.

Books to Improve Your Relationships

The 7th Floor Ain't Too High for Angels to Fly
*A Collection of Stories on Relationships &
Self-Understanding*
John M. Eades, Ph.D.

The individuals you meet in this provocative book
face moments of crucial insight, moments when life
changes irrevocably—for better or worse. Through
these tales of ordinary individuals in extraordinary circumstances, Eades helps you reflect on your own life
and invites you to discover the inner resources that lead
to true joy and fulfillment.
Code 3561 . . . . $10.95

Living in the Comfort Zone
The Gift of Boundaries in Relationships
Rokelle Lerner

This is one of the most useful books on relationships
you will ever read. It presents an honest, candid look at
individuals in relationships: to whom we are attracted
and why; how our initial relationship with our caregivers (parents) affects every relationship we have and
how we can overcome any lasting negative aspects;
how we can identify our current boundaries, identify
their weaknesses or insufficiencies, and transform them
so we can achieve the relationships we want and need.
It will improve and balance your life.
Code 3707 . . . . $9.95

We'd Have a Great Relationship
If It Weren't for You
Regaining Love and Intimacy Through Mutuality
Bruce Derman, Ph.D. with Michael Hauge

This book helps couples move beneath their surface
differences in order to recognize this basic truth: in any
committed relationship, both partners are the
same—absolutely equal in their capacity for love and
intimacy. It shows how this innovative process of
mutuality can replace drama and distance with light-
ness and joining, can greatly reduce the possibility of
divorce, and can transform restrictive sex lives into
ones that are expansive and free.
Code 3162 . . . . $12.95

Available at your favorite bookstore or call 1-800-441-5569 for Visa or
MasterCard orders. Prices do not include shipping and handling. Your
response code is HCI.